JAPANESE CULTURAL ENCOUNTERS
& HOW TO HANDLE THEM

HIROKO C. KATAOKA
with **TETSUYA KUSUMOTO**

PASSPORT BOOKS
a division of *NTC Publishing Group*
Lincolnwood, Illinois USA

Dedicated in memory of Robert O. Tilman

Published by Passport Books, a division of NTC Publishing Group.
©1991 by NTC Publishing Group, 4255 West Touhy Avenue,
Lincolnwood (Chicago), Illinois 60646-1975 U.S.A.
All rights reserved. No part of this book may be reproduced, stored
in a retrieval system, or transmitted in any form or by any means,
electronic, mechanical, photocopying, recording or otherwise, without
the prior permission of NTC Publishing Group.
Manufactured in the United States of America.

0 1 2 3 4 5 6 7 8 9 VP 9 8 7 6 5 4 3 2 1

CREDIT AND ACKNOWLEDGMENTS

Members of the Southeastern Association of Teachers of Japanese contributed some of the episodes and ideas for this book. (Some ideas were contributed by more than one person.) In addition to writing 26 of the episodes myself, I have edited the entire collection, which included the responsibility for selecting other writers' episodes and extensively revising many of them. In the process, there were a few members' contributions that did not remain in the final draft.

Tetsuya Kusumoto wrote 18 episodes (numbers 3, 4, 5, 9, 15, 16, 18, 19, 20, 23, 31, 35, 38, 40, 43, 45, 46, and 51) and offered editorial comments and suggestions for the other entries.

The following colleagues contributed to the final product—the numbers next to their names are the episodes that they wrote or suggested as concepts: Sam Coleman (numbers 25 and 33); Hiroko Goto (numbers 23, 26, and 45); Atsuko Hayashi (numbers 4 and 44); Kikuko Imamura (numbers 25 and 55); Toshiko Kishimoto (number 3); Yoshiko McCullough (numbers 39, 42, and 48); Mary Sisk (numbers 28 and 56); and Shigeko Uppuluri (number 7). Episode numbers not appearing in this list were exclusively mine.

I would like to thank Deborah Wyrick and James H. Holland II, for editing the first draft, and Akira Miura and Sam Coleman, who provided valuable perspectives and suggestions.

HOW TO USE THIS BOOK

This book contains 56 episodes of conflicts, problems, or embarrassing situations often encountered by Americans (especially "newcomers") in their interactions with the Japanese due to cultural differences between the United States and Japan. The episodes are divided into four sections: 1) Human Relations at Work and Leisure; 2) Etiquette, Formalities, and Customs; 3) Commonly Misused or Misunderstood Japanese Expressions; and 4) Handy Trivia. There is a question after each episode, followed by four possible answers to the question. Students should read each episode very carefully, then try to answer the question by choosing one of the four answers provided. After each answer, a page number is written; by turning to that page, the reader will find whether his or her answer was correct, along with an explanation. Reading and answering the shortest episode requires only a couple of minutes; the longer, complicated episodes may take more than five minutes, but not much longer.

To the Instructor

This book can be used as a textbook for the culture component of language study in the introductory Japanese language classroom either at the very beginning or end of each class period. If the class schedule is too tight to spare classroom time, students may be given one episode per day for homework, since each exercise requires only a few minutes and thus poses no burden to the student. In intermediate and advanced language classes, some of the episodes may provide topics for discussion in Japanese. The book can also be used in an introductory Japanese society and culture course as a discussion opener. It does not provide analytical insight or detailed information on Japanese culture, however, so other materials should be consulted for a more thorough investigation.

Although this book was originally designed for students of the Japanese language, episodes on that subject constitute only about one fourth of the situations because there are many good books on usages and misusages already available for those who want to study the language in depth. (The best, in my own judgment, is the *Nihongo Notes* series by Mizutani and Mizutani.) The episodes in this book that are related to language usage are limited to very basic phrases and sentences; many of them may be read by students in their third day of language study.

CONTENTS

PART I

Human Relations at Work and Leisure

1.   Apology

Tom rented a car one weekend. It was his first time driving a car in Japan, but he had been an excellent driver in the United States.

On his way to his friend's house, however, he had an accident. A young child about four years old ran into the street from an alley just as Tom was driving by. Tom was driving under the speed limit and he was watching the road carefully, so he stepped on the brakes immediately. However, the car did brush against the child, causing him to fall down. Tom immediately stopped the car and asked a passerby to call the police and an ambulance.

Fortunately, the child's injuries were minor. The police did not give Tom a ticket, and he was told that he was not at fault at all, thanks to some witnesses' reports. He felt sorry for the child but decided that there was nothing more he could do, so he tried to forget about the accident. However, after several days, Tom heard from the policeman that the child's parents were extremely upset about Tom's response to the incident.

Why were the child's parents upset?

A. They believed the police let Tom go too easily only because he was an American; Tom was, in fact, at fault. (See page 78.)

B. They were angry because Tom did not apologize to them, nor did he visit the child at the hospital, even though he was not at fault. Tom should have done those things to show his sincerity. (See page 64.)

C. Tom should have given the family money because a child was involved. In Japan, when one has an auto accident involving a child, the driver is supposed to pay a sizeable amount of "apology money," regardless of whose fault it is. (See page 105.)

D. They were egotistical people who could never admit they (and their family) could do any wrong. There are quite a few parents like that in Japan these days because of the social pressure to perform well; those who cannot live up to the expectations of their relatives and supervisors tend to suffer from this syndrome. (See page 115.)

2.   Browbeaten Husband?

Richard and his wife were sent to the Tokyo office of his company's joint venture partner for one year. Richard really liked his new position; his Japanese colleagues were dedicated and interesting, his boss was extremely competent, and the office had a pleasant atmosphere. He had heard, though, that his Japanese colleagues were socially very conservative. Richard was lucky enough to find an affordable home in a location about one hour's commute for him and convenient to shopping for his wife.

Richard also enjoyed going out after work with his colleagues about three times a week. Each time he did so, he called home to tell his wife that he'd be late because he was going out "with the guys." She was unhappy, however, because Richard's social life rarely included her. At one of these outings for drinks, his older colleagues joked that Richard was "tied to his wife's apron strings." (The actual, more graphic expression means that he is "sat upon" by his wife.)

Why did Richard's colleagues tease him about his wife?

A. Because Richard called his wife each time he went out with them. In Japan, men usually do not call their wives to tell them they'll be late. (See page 65.)

B. Because Richard's wife was unhappy whenever Richard went out with his workmates. In Japan, wives are not supposed to complain about anything their husbands do. (See page 117.)

C. Because Richard found a home in a location convenient for her but not too convenient for him. In Japan, a man's job is of paramount importance, so couples normally live near the husband's workplace even if the location is not convenient for the wife. (See page 72.)

D. Because Richard brought his wife with him to Japan. In Japan, men normally leave their wives behind if their foreign assignments are as short as one year. (See page 98.)

3.   Club Activities

When Sally went to Japan for a junior-year-abroad program, she heard that extracurricular activities were very popular in Japanese universities, so she decided to join a club. Since she had always been interested in Japanese martial arts, she joined the Aikido Club. Sally enjoyed Aikido very much and she also liked her fellow club members. However, she soon found out that club activities were not limited to regular practice on campus: the members often went out drinking together, had parties, went to camp for training, and organized events for an all-school festival held once every year. Sally was reluctant to participate in some of these activities, especially parties held at local bars. She did not enjoy drinking with the club members because she often felt compelled to drink more than she wanted, or to sing songs. But she also knew that refusing to do these things might make her seem aloof and unfriendly.

Sally, like most other Americans, found it difficult to accept such social obligations. It almost seemed to her that all the members of a group were expected to behave and even "think" the same way in Japanese society, whether they liked it or not.

Regardless of how Sally decides to solve her problem, what would help her understand why her fellow club members seem so dedicated to their group activities?

A. Aikido is a martial art, and martial arts devotees are supposed to do everything together, particularly drinking and carousing in the samurai tradition. (See page 111.)

B. It's all an effort to treat Sally specially, as a foreign guest member. (See page 96.)

C. Social activities *do* play a more important part in the life of the typical Japanese college student than in the United States. (See page 87.)

D. The Japanese are always group oriented as an ingrained trait. (See page 69.)

4

4. Compliment (1)

One day Jane talked with her advisor, Professor Hashimoto, about the book he had recently written in English concerning various aspects of Japanese culture. The book had just received very favorable reviews from both the academic and the popular press. When Jane read his book, she was impressed by his unique analysis of Japanese culture; his arguments were both understandable and convincing. Other people who read the book felt the same way Jane did, including Jane's friend Masako, who was Professor Hashimoto's assistant. Jane told Professor Hashimoto how wonderful his book was: she said, "Sensee no hon wa tottemo yokatta desu. Kanshin shimashita" ("Your book was very good. I was impressed."). As Jane left the professor's office, though, Masako came out of the office and whispered in her ear, "I've got to tell you something about compliments to social superiors!"

What do you think Masako wanted to tell Jane about her compliment?

A. Jane's compliment sounded sarcastic to Professor Hashimoto because his book was not that good. (See page 113.)

B. Jane's Japanese was grammatically wrong, so Professor Hashimoto did not understand her. (See page 110.)

C. Professor Hashimoto didn't want to hear a hackneyed compliment such as the one Jane gave. He wanted a concrete critique. (See page 91.)

D. The way Jane complimented Professor Hashimoto was culturally inappropriate. Professor Hashimoto felt his academic ability and work were being "evaluated" by the student. In Japanese society such evaluation by someone at a lower academic level is not allowed. (See page 82.)

5. Denying a Compliment

Larry came to Japan to teach conversational English at a small private school in Tokyo. One day he went to a party held at one of his students' homes. He spoke English with his students there. They were from a beginner's class, but Larry found their English was fairly good; he praised each of them for their command of English. He expected that they would reply with "Thank you," but all of them refused to accept his compliment. Instead they smiled pleasantly and commented on how much they had yet to learn.

Later, one of them played the guitar and sang a song. Larry praised the student's performance. The student looked embarrassed and denied the compliment, but he smiled and played an encore! As Larry was leaving, he thanked the hostess for the meal and told her that she was a good cook. The hostess seemed pleased, but she too gave a negative reply to the compliment, saying that she would prefer serving something nicer to a foreign guest but her abilities were limited. Larry thought it odd and vaguely disappointing that none of the Japanese at the party responded positively to his compliments.

What should Larry do next time he's favorably impressed by something that Japanese acquaintances do?

A. He should compliment Japanese acquaintances, but then add something critical to "beat them to the punch." (See page 101.)

B. He should avoid making compliments because they're just not recognized among the Japanese. (See page 113.)

C. He should stop making compliments; Japanese know how to compliment one another, but a foreigner could never sense how and when to make an effective compliment. (See page 67.)

D. He should not be discouraged from making sincere compliments, but he should expect contradictory replies because a direct acceptance of the compliment would indicate immodesty. (See page 100.)

6.   Flower Class

Cindy, a student spending a year in Japan, decided to take a course in flower arrangement. Her host mother recommended studying with an acquaintance of hers who gave flower-arranging lessons. Upon meeting the woman, Cindy feared she would not be an effective teacher because she did not seem to be lively or gregarious. Cindy decided to attend the woman's class anyway because her host mother had recommended her, and she did not know anyone else who taught flower arrangement.

Cindy's apprehensiveness grew during the first few lessons. The teacher made an arrangement; then the students tried to imitate it. Cindy created a different arrangement and wanted to get the teacher's opinion. The teacher stopped Cindy and started to reshape the materials into the original. Grudgingly, Cindy thought she had better copy her teacher's arrangement, this time, at least. She had trouble with the angles of the main flowers, so she asked the teacher, "At what angle should this stem be standing?" The teacher looked surprised but answered, "I really don't know." Getting irritated, Cindy asked her if she could draw the design on a sheet of paper so she could figure out the angles and remember the design. The teacher looked even more surprised and answered again, "I don't know."

What's the moral of this story?

A. Follow your instinct. Cindy didn't like the teacher from the start; she should have looked for another teacher then. (See page 93.)

B. In Japan, you may have to endure some unpleasant situations because you can't let others lose face. Cindy could not get out of the class because the teacher was her host mother's friend. (See page 85.)

C. All traditional art in Japan is taught this way. (See page 76.)

D. The teacher should pay attention to Cindy's efforts and questions; by so doing, she might become a better teacher. Japanese people have always learned from other cultures, and this teacher should use the opportunity to learn from a student familiar with Western teaching methods. (See page 90.)

7. Gift (1)

Kim went on a three-week trip to Japan to visit some friends. One day Yuko, who once was Kim's roommate in the United States, took Kim to visit her uncle. Mr. Uemura, Yuko's uncle, lived in a fairly large, traditional house with his wife, his children, and his mother. The house was filled with beautiful crafts. Mr. Uemura said that his mother had been taking arts and crafts lessons and had filled the house with dolls, tapestries, wall-hangings, and baskets. Kim pointed to two dolls she particularly liked and complimented Mr. Uemura's mother on her lovely work. Mr. Uemura's mother smiled happily, took them off the shelf, and told Kim that they were hers to keep. Surprised and embarrassed, Kim declined the offer, although she truly loved the dolls. Mrs. Uemura, however, insisted that Kim should take them back with her.

What should Kim do?

A. Do not accept them. Mrs. Uemura was just trying to be polite, expecting that Kim would not take them. (See page 107.)

B. Accept them with many thanks since there is no other way out of the situation. Remember, though, that if you vociferously praise or admire a personal possession as some Americans tend to do, the owner may want to please you so much that he or she will insist on giving it to you. (See page 92.)

C. Accept them but offer to pay a reasonable amount, enough to cover the materials that Mrs. Uemura had to buy. (See page 80.)

D. Ask the price of the dolls. If they are not too expensive, accept them. (See page 103.)

8.   Honest Person

At a party in California, John met a new Japanese student, Tadashi. They talked about their families, trips they had taken, and their life as college students. John figured out that Tadashi's family was quite well-to-do: according to Tadashi, each of his four brothers and sisters had gone to an American or European college for a year or so; Tadashi also said he was living in an apartment that John knew was in the most exclusive part of town. Tadashi sounded like an interesting person, and John wanted to become friends with him. John was hesitant, however, because he suspected that Tadashi was lying about his family and his life since Tadashi never looked into John's eyes as he talked.

Is John's suspicion well founded?

A. Yes. The fact that Tadashi never looked into John's eyes indicates that Tadashi is a liar. (See page 70.)

B. Yes. The fact that Tadashi didn't look into John's eyes is irrelevant, but Tadashi is an untrustworthy braggart. Even the richest Japanese families do not spoil their children by buying expensive things for them. At best, Tadashi must be exaggerating. (See page 75.)

C. No. Among Japanese it's impolite and sometimes even aggressive to look into people's eyes, and Tadashi, who just arrived in the United States, simply followed his previous training. His statements could certainly be true because some well-to-do families in any country lavish gifts and cash upon their children. (See page 118.)

D. No. Tadashi happens to be cross-eyed (strabismic), which is a fairly common trait among Japanese males. (See page 66.)

9.   Hugging

After an hour and a half flight from Tokyo, Meg and her good friend, Yoko Yamada, arrived at an airport near Yoko's home town in the northern part of Japan. Yoko had invited Meg to stay with her family during the summer vacation. Meg thought that Yoko's parents would be excited to see their daughter because she had been in the United States for the last two years; and she expected a typical scene of hugs and kisses as Yoko was reunited with her parents.

When Meg and Yoko left the baggage claim area, they found Yoko's parents waiting for them. Yoko approached them and said, "Tadaima" ("I'm home!"). Then her parents said, "Okaeri. Tsukareta deshoo" ("Welcome back home. You must be tired"). They were all smiling and acting happy, but Meg was surprised to see that they only exchanged a few words and that they didn't hug in spite of the fact that they hadn't seen each other for two whole years! In fact, when Jane looked around the lobby, she didn't see any other Japanese people hugging, either.

Meg was welcomed warmly by Yoko's parents, but she began to wonder if the Japanese are actually cold, emotionless people.

Why do you think Yoko's parents didn't hug their daughter?

A. Yoko and her parents hadn't been getting along well lately, so her parents were not overly happy about their daughter's return. (See page 73.)

B. Yoko's parents were mad at Yoko because she had brought Meg. In accordance with Japanese custom, they wanted to meet Yoko alone to enjoy the happy moment without having to worry about a stranger. (See page 115.)

C. Japanese people usually do not hug and kiss each other in public. Such open displays of affection are perceived as embarrassing, perhaps even scandalous. (See page 94.)

D. Yoko's parents are such shy people that they can't hug their daughter in front of others. (See page 89.)

10.   Letter from Parents

One day, about three months after Jane arrived in Japan, the International Student Program at her university gave a reception for foreign students and their "home-stay" families, who provided lodging and meals for a nominal amount. At the reception Jane overheard her host mother complaining to Jane's Japanese advisor in Japanese that they had not yet heard from Jane's American family. When the host mother started expressing her concern over Jane and her parents' relationship, Jane thought she should stop eavesdropping and leave the room. Jane didn't even know that her host mother expected a letter from her parents; no one in the host family had mentioned it to her, and Jane got along very well with all the members of the host family. Frustrated, she wished her Japanese were good enough to tell her host mother that she was an independent person who could handle her own life, and that her parents had nothing to do with her living arrangement in Japan.

Why was Jane's host mother complaining to the advisor?

A. Jane's host mother wanted to consult with Jane's parents, because she was causing problems in the host family's daily life. (See page 83.)

B. It is customary in Japan for a college student's parents to write a thank-you letter to the host family. (See page 114.)

C. Jane's host mother is overly concerned and, perhaps, somewhat meddlesome. (See page 68.)

D. Jane's host mother had written to her parents but did not receive a reply; she thought Jane's parents had disowned their daughter. (See page 84.)

11.   Misbehaving Children

Michiko invited Susan to come for tea one afternoon. It was the first time Susan had ever been invited to a Japanese home, so she was very excited. Michiko, with her five-year-old son, Kazuo, greeted Susan. Michiko and Susan talked over a cup of tea and some cake. Susan enjoyed herself, although she was disturbed by the way Michiko let Kazuo bring all his toys into the living room and make a mess. But then, Susan thought, some American parents let their kids join the adults once in a while; besides, Michiko's apartment was so small that there was no other room in which Kazuo could play comfortably. Susan's thinking changed when Kazuo started screaming at the top of his lungs. Susan had read how well-behaved Japanese children are at school, so this behavior surprised her. Susan was even more shocked when all Michiko did was to talk gently to Kazuo: "Kazuo, you're such a good boy, so be quiet, please. Let's go upstairs and take a nap, OK, Kazuo?" After a few minutes, Susan's patience was about to snap.

What should Susan do at this point?

A.   Nothing. Japanese children are not expected to behave themselves at home as they are at school, and Japanese parents exhibit more tolerance of tantrums than do Americans, especially in front of guests. It is not Susan's business to discipline Kazuo, so she should endure the situation until Michiko resolves it. (See page 116.)

B.   Michiko obviously does not know how badly Kazuo behaves. Susan should advise Michiko that Kazuo should learn to behave himself, or else Michiko and Kazuo will be embarrassed when Kazuo reaches school age. (See page 71.)

C.   Kazuo's behavior is intolerable to anyone. Susan should spank him; Michiko would appreciate Susan's help, since Michiko herself is having trouble dealing with Kazuo. (See page 79.)

D.   Susan should try to ignore Kazuo and end her association with Michiko. Something is wrong with Michiko if she tolerates Kazuo's outrageous behavior. (See page 104.)

12.   Noisy Neighbor

Susan, who lives in a small apartment in Tokyo, enjoys listening to music. One Sunday afternoon, Susan was listening to some new records. After a while, her doorbell rang. It was Mrs. Kawakami, a housewife living next door to Susan. Her husband was an ambitious businessman in a leading company. Mrs. Kawakami apologetically told Susan that her husband was sick with a terrible headache, and she politely asked Susan to turn down the stereo so he could rest. Susan was a little disappointed, but she understood Mr. Kawakami's situation. So Susan turned off the stereo, told Mrs. Kawakami to give Mr. Kawakami her regards, and decided to spend the day reading.

The next day, Susan ran into Mr. Kawakami as she was walking home from the train station. She asked him if he had recovered from his headache and was shocked to hear his reply: "What headache? I haven't had a headache for years! I don't have too many things I can be proud of, but my health is one."

Why did Mrs. Kawakami tell Susan that Mr. Kawakami was sick?

A. Mrs. Kawakami was annoyed by the stereo—maybe it was a little too loud—but she was afraid that a straightforward complaint might jeopardize her relationship with Susan. (See page 86.)

B. Mrs. Kawakami suffers from paranoia, which is very common among Japanese housewives living in apartments. Their husbands, whose lives are dedicated to their companies, ignore their wives completely, so many housewives start imagining that their husbands are sick at home. (See page 112.)

C. Mr. Kawakami was lying. As a striving Japanese businessman, he did not want anyone to find out that he was sick. He was concerned that he would lose out on promotions, should his superiors at the company learn about his illness. (See page 106.)

D. Mrs. Kawakami was a mean woman who enjoyed interrupting other people's pleasurable activities, so she lied about her husband's health. (See page 77.)

13.   Personal Questions

Kate was invited to a meeting of the ESS (English-Speaking Society) at a nearby company. Since she always appreciated Japanese visitors to her Japanese class in the United States, she was happy for the opportunity to help Japanese people.

There were about ten people, mostly young men, in the room. At first they were all quiet, but as they became relaxed, they started asking Kate questions. They asked her where she was from, how many brothers and sisters she had, what her job was, why she came to Japan, and how she liked the country. After a while, the questions became more personal: they asked how old Kate was, and whether she was married. When Kate answered no to the latter question, the Japanese asked whether she was engaged to be married, when she wanted to be married, and whether her job paid well. Kate started becoming angry and wondered what had become of the politeness and thoughtfulness she had thought were characteristic of Japanese people.

Why did the ESS members ask such personal questions?

A. Young Japanese people these days are not polite. The good old days are gone. (See page 119.)

B. Kate just happened to get stuck with an inconsiderate, aggressive group of people. She shouldn't judge all Japanese from this particular group. (See page 109.)

C. Many Japanese people do not consider such questions overly personal. They do not expect precise answers, either. (See page 88.)

D. The young men were interested in dating her. They wouldn't ask such questions if she were not an attractive young woman. (See page 92.)

14.   Secretary

John, a student of Japanese, recently met Mayumi, a Japanese exchange student studying at his university. They became friends quickly. Mayumi, majoring in political science, seemed to be a bright woman with fairly liberal ideas about women and life in general. She spoke English very well, too, and John found out that she attended a well-known and respected college in Japan. One day he asked her about her future career plans. Mayumi answered that she hoped to become a secretary in one of Japan's leading trading companies. Surprised, John asked again if this was really what she wanted to do, because he thought she should be able to get a better position than that with a college degree, political science training, and experience living in the United States. Mayumi gave him a puzzled look and asked him if he didn't think she could do the job.

Why do you think Mayumi wanted to be a secretary?

A. In Japan, where women are regarded as incapable of doing anything important, becoming a secretary is the best career Mayumi could hope for. (See page 108.)

B. "Secretaries" in Japan are different from those in the United States. More like executive administrative assistants, they have fairly responsible and well-paying jobs in large companies. The term "secretary" is a mistranslation. (See page 95.)

C. Although Mayumi seemed to have high aspirations and liberal ideas, she was in fact very traditional. She believed a secretarial job is a proper position for a woman. (See page 97.)

D. John misunderstood Mayumi because her pronunciation was bad. She actually said "secret," not "secretary," concerning her career plan. (See page 102.)

15.   Self-Defense

One morning, at the Japanese company where Bob worked part-time, he took a finished document to his boss's office. His boss checked the document very carefully and pointed out a critical mistake in it. He also told him that the document should have been submitted earlier.

The document was late because Bob hadn't had access to the word-processor at the office until very recently. As for the mistake in the document, Bob noticed that it was made by a colleague of his, and not by him. Bob explained these things to his boss calmly and very politely in Japanese, showing that he was not at fault. Having listened to Bob, the boss looked displeased and suddenly said to him in English, "I don't want to hear such excuses. Do this again, and give it to me before you go home today!"

Bob left the boss's office, feeling upset. He didn't understand why his boss had become offended since he had done nothing wrong. Bob didn't know what to do.

Why do you think Bob's boss got mad at Bob?

A. Bob made an excuse and failed to apologize. Apologies are very important in Japan. (See page 81.)

B. Bob's approach was very rude because he defended himself to his boss and implied criticism of his colleague. (See page 83.)

C. Bob's boss was bullying him, an example of traditional Japanese xenophobia. (See page 110.)

D. Part-time workers in Japan are in a particularly low-status position and are not allowed to talk back to their superiors. (See page 107.)

16.   Staff Meeting

Alan, a business intern at a Japanese company, was looking forward to attending his first staff meeting. Since the agenda included an issue that would be controversial in an American office, Alan expected to encounter an interesting discussion.

The meeting, however, ended up being pretty dull: there were no pro and con arguments. Instead, people asked a few questions about the issue, and some made brief comments in favor of one proposed solution. Alan had heard that some of the staff disagreed with this proposed solution but they merely raised a few minor questions. One committee member did state his objection; there was a moment of silence, and no one responded. Then the chairperson asked if there were any other questions or comments and brought the issue to a close. He didn't even call for a vote! In the end, Alan thought, they hadn't discussed anything substantial at all.

Why do you think the staff members were relatively quiet at the meeting and voiced little dissent?

A.   They didn't have anything to say because the subject had nothing to do with them. (See page 64.)

B.   Japanese don't know how to discuss issues because discussion is a relatively new concept in Japan. (See page 93.)

C.   Japanese people rarely discuss issues because everything is decided by a single authority. (See page 66.)

D.   They had decided to avoid open confrontation in this instance, or probably they knew that the issue had been settled beforehand. (See page 75.)

17.   Terrible Son

Bob's family has been hosting a Japanese exchange student, Tomio, for about 6 months. Tomio is a model guest and a model student: he gets along with everyone in the family, he helps the family with household chores, he is outgoing and has made numerous friends, and he receives excellent grades at school. He has truly been a joy for the entire family.

One day Tomio's father visited Bob's family during a business trip to the United States. He thanked Bob's parents for taking care of his son, who "couldn't do anything himself, has very bad manners, and is selfish." He even apologized that he and his wife had not done a good job of bringing up their son to be a gentleman like Bob. When Bob's parents disagreed with these criticisms and praised Tomio, Tomio's father looked really embarrassed and apologized even more about his "stupid and terrible son." Tomio, however, was smiling as his father was saying horrible things about him! Bob started to get angry with Tomio's father and wondered what was wrong.

What was wrong? Why did Tomio's father say such things?

A.   At home in Japan, Tomio was actually what his father described. Japanese youngsters are expected to behave outside of the home to avoid *haji* or shame to the family name. (See page 103.)

B.   Tomio's father had extremely high standards for his son: unless the son behaved absolutely perfectly, he would not recognize his son's accomplishments at all. This type of parenting is not unusual in Japan, where everyone strives for upward social mobility through self-improvement. (See page 72.)

C.   Tomio used to be what his father described, but his life in the U.S. has changed him completely. An international experience has a beneficial effect on many young people. (See page 100.)

D.   Tomio's father really doesn't believe what he says. In his heart he knows that Tomio is an outstanding young man, and he is very proud of his son. Japanese people often show their respect to others by humbling themselves, however, and this often takes the form of denigrating themselves and their family members. (See page 111.)

18.　Undecided

Phyllis works in a Japanese company. She and her section chief were discussing her proposal for improving work conditions that she had written up and submitted to him a month earlier. As they talked, Phyllis became frustrated because her section chief seemed noncommittal. Instead of concentrating on the specifics of her plan about the budgetary problems involved, he talked vaguely and about what other people in the section would think. Phyllis felt this was irrelevant because he had the authority to control the budget and to make decisions without depending on subordinates. When Phyllis asked him if he would accept her proposal, he said, "I'll think about it." Then he changed the subject.

Later Phyllis heard from a colleague that the section chief had turned down her proposal. She wondered why the section chief had not told her directly that the plan would not be implemented.

Why do you think the section chief was so noncommittal during their initial conversation?

A.　The section chief was not sure if money could be allocated or if he could win the consensus of other people in the section. (See page 87.)

B.　The section chief didn't like Phyllis, so even if her proposal was good, he didn't want to accept it. (See page 106.)

C.　The section chief was seriously considering Phyllis's proposal but could not come to a decision. (See page 98.)

D.　The section chief actually didn't want to accept Phyllis's proposal. He hoped Phyllis would understand that his hesitancy indicated his rejection of the proposal. (See page 67.)

19. Upperclassmen

Becky is a student at a Japanese university. Becky always tries to be friendly and courteous. She is also very careful about her language usage: when she talks to older people or strangers, she uses "formal" style speech; she uses the "informal" style when she talks to other college students and to her host family members. However, her closest Japanese friend keeps telling her that she should use the formal style when addressing *senpai* (people who have been affiliated with the group—whether it be a club, a school, or a company—longer than she has; in most cases they are older than her) of the club she belongs to, too. Becky doesn't understand why—they are only one or two years older than she is. They are students too, and some of them are her friends! Becky is beginning to wonder if she can trust her best friend's advice.

Would listening to her friend help Becky in her relations with the other club members?

A. No, because foreigners are always outsiders anyway; they can't be accepted as in-group members in Japanese society no matter how politely they speak. (See page 69.)

B. Yes, because one shouldn't talk in informal style to older people who aren't part of one's own family even if they are only one or two years older. (See page 107.)

C. No. These people don't know how to react to Becky because the Japanese are not used to the American style of friendliness. Becky is bound to feel disappointed no matter what she does. (See page 83.)

D. Yes. Women are supposed to talk politely and relatively formally in Japanese society, so Becky shouldn't talk informally to her *senpai*. Neither should she use informal style to any men her own age. (See page 109.)

PART II

Etiquette, Formalities, and Customs

20. Blowing One's Nose

Mr. Brown, who had recently come to Japan on business, visited his daughter's host family, the Uedas. His daughter was studying at a Japanese university in a one-year home-stay program. Mr. Brown was welcomed by the host family and entertained with refreshments. When talking over a cup of tea, he felt his nose tickle. He took his handkerchief out of the pocket and blew his nose. Then he noticed that the host family looked disturbed for a moment. Mr. Brown didn't give it much thought at that time. He enjoyed his time with the host family and left.

The next day, Mr. Brown attended a meeting with Japanese businessmen. He noticed again that some people looked askance at him when he blew his nose with his handkerchief.

Why do you think Japanese people looked disconcerted when Mr. Brown blew his nose?

A. It is rude in Japan to blow one's nose when drinking or eating. (See page 76.)

B. Japanese people usually do not blow their noses in front of others, and they never blow their noses with a cloth handkerchief. (See page 101.)

C. Mr. Brown blew his nose very noisily, which disturbed Japanese people. (See page 119.)

D. Japanese people never blow their noses. (See page 113.)

21. Calling Card

Jeff is an American student studying in Japan. His course of study includes a part-time internship in a market research company. The first day he went to the company, everyone welcomed him. When they introduced themselves and found out that Jeff had a difficult time remembering Japanese names, they all gave him their *meishi,* or business cards, after they wrote down their names in English on the back. After thanking them for their kindness, Jeff wrote some notes on each card, put the *meishi* in his wallet, and thanked them all. Then Jeff put the wallet in his back pocket. Somehow, at that point everyone fell awkwardly silent for a moment, as if they were unpleasantly surprised.

What caused the sudden silence?

A. Jeff should not have written on the *meishi* or put them in his back pocket. (See page 112.)

B. Jeff should have thanked his Japanese colleagues for their name cards more politely than he did. (See page 69.)

C. Jeff should have politely declined the *meishi* and, instead, have tried to memorize his co-workers' names, even if it was difficult; Japanese people always appreciate Westerners who make a special effort to accommodate themselves to new situations. (See page 74.)

D. Jeff should have known all the *kanji,* the pictographic characters used in Japanese writing, so his Japanese colleagues would not have had to provide English for him. (See page 105.)

22.   Coat

Cathy is an American housewife who has been taking Japanese at a nearby university. One cold winter day, she decided to invite Keiko, the wife of a new faculty member recently arrived from Japan, to lunch at a cozy restaurant that specialized in soup. Cathy called Keiko that morning and invited her in Japanese; Keiko happily accepted the invitation. Although Cathy suggested she'd pick up Keiko and they'd go to the restaurant together from Keiko's house, Keiko said she'd come to Cathy's house, because Cathy's house was closer to the restaurant. Cathy's doorbell rang right on time, and she found Keiko standing at the doorstep with her coat on her arm, looking very cold. Cathy invited Keiko into the living room, wondering what her next step should be.

What should Cathy do at this point?

A. Serve Keiko some hot tea, talk with her for about 30 minutes, then go out. It is a Japanese custom to have tea before going out to eat, and Keiko assumed it was the same in the United States. (See page 102.)

B. Keiko thought that they were having lunch at Cathy's place. Cathy should apologize politely for the misunderstanding and let Keiko know that they are going out. (See page 65.)

C. Cathy should interpret Keiko's removing her coat as a sign that she didn't want to go to the restaurant. Cathy should quickly fix some lunch at home instead. (See page 114.)

D. Act as if nothing is wrong and go out to lunch immediately. Cathy should ignore the fact that Keiko has taken off her coat. (See page 70.)

23.   Conversational Drag

Fred called Mr. Sato to hear Mr. Sato's response to an important business deal that Fred had skillfully arranged with Mr. Sato's help. Mr. Sato was an enthusiastic partner in the deal. Fred was bothered, however, by Mr. Sato's habit of interjecting questions into the conversation. He would say, "Hello, hello, do you hear me?" or "Hello, hello, do you understand?" as if Fred were neither very bright nor very attentive.

What made Mr. Sato continually interrupt with such questions?

A. It was a poor telephone connection. Phones in Japan are notoriously bad. (See page 118.)

B. Fred had the bad habit of letting his mind wander during dull conversation. Americans also had to keep asking him if he was listening. (See page 104.)

C. Fred didn't respond frequently to Mr. Sato. Mr. Sato expected feedback from Fred to make sure he was listening and was actively engaged in the discussion. (See page 73.)

D. It was the first time that Mr. Sato had talked with a foreigner on the phone, and he was extremely tense. (See page 85.)

24.   Decision Making

John invited his Japanese classmate Kenji, who recently arrived from Japan, to join him at his parents' home for Thanksgiving dinner. As soon as they arrived, John's parents asked Kenji if he wanted something to drink, to which Kenji responded, "No thank you." Right before dinner they asked again what he wanted to drink, offering him wine, milk, orange juice, apple juice, and beer. His answer this time was "Anything will be fine." Not knowing what to do, John's mother poured some wine, water, and apple juice. Kenji drank the apple juice and water eventually, so John's mother asked again if he wanted anything else to drink. Again Kenji's answer was a "no thank you." Kenji ended up eating dessert without any drink.

Why did Kenji respond so vaguely and confusingly to offers of drinks?

A. It is not appropriate to specify one's wants as a first-time guest to those whom one does not know well. Kenji was simply being polite. (See page 77.)

B. In Japan it is bad manners to drink before or after dinner; only during dinner is one supposed to drink anything. (See page 90.)

C. Japanese are an indecisive people. Since he cannot make up his mind, he says "no thank you" to avoid having to make decisions. (See page 92.)

D. Kenji simply was not at all thirsty. (See page 64.)

25.   Drinks

Leo was in his sixth week of a one-year internship at the central research laboratory of a Japanese electronics company. His section chief, Mr. Okamura, invited him out for drinks along with a few Japanese co-workers who were his age. First they went to a traditional-looking bar where they drank sake. Mr. Okamura poured drinks for everyone, so Leo frequently pushed his sake cup over for a refill. Then one of Leo's co-workers poured, so Leo pushed his cup in his direction. Mr. Okamura paid the bill, but the evening wasn't over! They then went to a small bar with a *karaoke,* an audio system that provides amateur singers with musical accompaniment and electronic effects that make their voices sound professional (in theory, at least!). After everyone had been drinking for a while, they began singing at the microphone. When Mr. Okamura asked Leo to sing, Leo poured himself another drink, walked to the microphone, and belted out "Love Me Tender." Next morning, Mr. Okamura smiled broadly when he saw Leo and said, "Let's go drinking again soon. And this time I'll show you something about drinking like a true Japanese."

What will Mr. Okamura tell Leo to do differently?

A.   Leo should have paid the bills. Newcomers are always expected to pay at least for the first round of drinks. (See page 66.)

B.   Leo's singing at the *karaoke* was a sure sign that he'd gone beyond his limits, which offends most Japanese men. Mr. Okamura will probably lecture him about this. (See page 81.)

C.   Because they were drinking alcoholic beverages, Leo should have held his glass when someone else poured for him, and he should have poured the other person's drink in return. Pouring your own drink is not appropriate in such social drinking sessions, either. (See page 109.)

D.   Leo had made a shameless pass at the *karaoke* bar hostess, which embarrassed Mr. Okamura. When they next go out, they will make a point of apologizing to her. (See page 74.)

26.   Eating

Tom was at the dinner table for the first time with his new host family. His host mother, Mrs. Yoshida, was a good cook, and there was plenty of food on the table. Tom enjoyed the meal as well as the pleasant conversation. He ate so much that he felt absolutely stuffed. When he said, "Tottemo oishikatta desu. Gochisoosama deshita" ("It was delicious. Thank you for the meal."), both host parents insisted that he eat more, saying, "Mada takusan arimasu kara, motto doozo" ("There is plenty more, so please eat more."). Tom declined their offer very politely by saying he had had enough, but they insisted again. Tom was dismayed but he felt hesitant about resisting their offer. He put more food on his plate and finished it somehow.

Why did Tom end up eating more than he wanted?

A. It is customary in Japan for hosts to insist on their guests' taking more. Tom didn't have to eat extra food if he didn't want any more. (See page 110.)

B. It is a Japanese custom to finish all the food on the dinner table. Tom's host parents wanted him to have his share since there was still so much food left. (See page 67.)

C. Tom's pronunciation was clumsy. His host parents didn't understand what he said. (See page 86.)

D. Tom should have automatically declined the offer of more food repeatedly (even if he were still hungry!). In Japan, guests never eat "seconds"; when offered more food, Japanese people always firmly but politely decline. (See page 108.)

27.   Farewells

Mr. Young and his family have been sent to Japan on a long-term business assignment. Mr. Young's company subsidized a fairly large house since they knew the Youngs had a large family. One evening the Youngs invited the Yamashitas, Mr. Young's colleague and his family, to dinner at their home. The Yamashitas seemed to enjoy the American dinner Mrs. Young cooked for them, and the children enjoyed one another's company too. The language barrier caused a few awkward moments, but in general everyone talked, laughed, and ate a lot. Around 10:30, the Yamashitas said that they had to go soon so they could catch the bus home. The two families promised to get together again, and the Yamashitas walked out the door. After saying good-bye, the Youngs closed the door and started washing the dishes.

The next morning at work Mr. Yamashita thanked Mr. Young for the dinner. Mr. Yamashita sounded strangely formal, and he then apologized profusely for staying so late. Mr. Young felt surprised, and he wondered why Mr. Yamashita should be apologetic when the Youngs had actually wanted him and his family to stay longer.

Why did Mr. Yamashita assume that he and his family had overstayed?

A.   According to Japanese custom, the Yamashitas should have left by nine o'clock at the latest. (See page 84.)

B.   The Yamashitas were jealous of the large house the Youngs have, and Mr. Yamashita was being passive–aggressive in his apologies. (See page 99.)

C.   Some of the awkward moments they had experienced were actually quite taxing for the Yamashitas. Japanese people tend to hide their feelings, so the Yamashitas tried to look as if they were having a good time. By 10:30, they were exhausted. (See page 115.)

D.   Mr. Yamashita felt that his family must have stayed too long because the Youngs closed the door immediately after the Yamashitas walked out of the house. (See page 80.)

28.   Flowers (1)

Sarah was doing temporary consulting work with a Japanese company. Rie, the secretary for one of the top managers, spoke excellent English and had been acting as liaison for Sarah. Sarah was very grateful to Rie, who had in fact gone well beyond the call of duty in taking care of Sarah. On her way to the office one morning, Sarah spontaneously decided to give Rie some flowers. When she handed the four red carnations she had selected to Rie, however, Rie looked shocked.

Why was Rie disturbed?

A. Since four is an unlucky number in Japan, Sarah should have given Rie either one, two, three, or five flowers. (See page 91.)

B. Rie would have appreciated any other color flower, but red flowers are only given to the families of recently deceased persons. (See page 108.)

C. Women never give each other flowers in Japan. A gift of flowers conveys a romantic message, and Rie was afraid her office mates would laugh when she told them who gave her the bouquet. (See page 71.)

D. Rie was afraid her superiors would be angry with her if she accepted the flowers. (See page 79.)

29.   Gift (2)

For a couple of months, Mindy has been teaching English to Mr. Takeda, a Japanese businessman, on Saturdays. On the 26th of December, Mrs. Takeda came to Mindy's apartment without any notice. Mindy was in a panic because she had not dressed properly to see a visitor, but she managed to keep her dignity by looking as if nothing was wrong. Saying that she just came to deliver a gift and that she did not intend to stay, Mrs. Takeda took out a heavy box wrapped in a very pretty sheet of paper. She also apologized for not having come sooner. Mindy, who assumed it was a late Christmas gift, thanked Mrs. Takeda very politely and asked her if it would be all right to open it. Mrs. Takeda looked surprised and uncomfortable, but gave her consent. Mindy opened the box and found a can of fancy cooking oil. She was a little disappointed and wondered why Mrs. Takeda would bring such a gift, but she politely thanked Mrs. Takeda again and said that it was exactly what she needed. Nevertheless, Mrs. Takeda still looked uncomfortable.

What was the source of this discomfort?

A. Mrs. Takeda made a mistake and brought the wrong package. The cooking oil was not a gift to Mindy. (See page 117.)

B. It wasn't a Christmas gift. It was a thank-you gift for Mindy's help to her husband, so Mindy shouldn't have opened it then. (See page 89.)

C. Mindy should have changed her clothes. Mrs. Takeda was uncomfortable seeing Mindy in her old clothes. (See page 75.)

D. Mrs. Takeda was embarrassed about bringing the Christmas gift one day late. (See page 94.)

30. Gift (3)

Mary, a college student, was going to be visited by Mrs. Yokoyama, a well-to-do, middle-aged Japanese housewife who wanted to learn English from her. Their common friend, Mrs. Ikeda, had suggested Mary as a tutor to Mrs. Yokoyama. Since it was to be their first meeting, Mary was concerned about the impression she would make; she had put on a nice pair of pants and had cleaned her apartment thoroughly. When Mrs. Yokoyama arrived, Mary greeted her properly (she even bowed correctly!) and showed her into the one-room apartment. As soon as they sat down, Mrs. Yokoyama took out a box nicely wrapped with paper from a famous bakery. Since Mary knew that it is customary in Japan to bring a small gift when one visits someone's home, she gracefully took the box with her left hand. When Mrs. Yokoyama left, she said she would contact Mary later to discuss the details of their tutoring arrangement.

Later Mary heard from Mrs. Ikeda that Mrs. Yokoyama was hesitant about having Mary as her tutor, because she thought Mary may not be able to teach "high-class" (*joohin na*) English, judging from her behavior.

What behavior of Mary's caused Mrs. Yokoyama to come to that conclusion?

A. Mary should not have worn pants, even if they were the best pair she had. (See page 95.)

B. It's her choice of apartment. Young women from proper families should not rent a one-room apartment. (See page 116.)

C. Mary should not have extended her left hand to receive the gift. The left hand is used only when touching something unclean. (See page 82.)

D. Mary should not have extended one arm; it's better to extend both arms to receive gifts. (See page 93.)

31.   Greetings

One morning John was walking on the campus of the Japanese university he was attending. He saw Professor Saito talking with someone. John approached him and greeted him with a smile: "Ohayoo gozaimasu" ("Good morning!"). Professor Saito returned the greeting and introduced him to Mr. Tanaka, who was a graduate of that university and now worked for a Japanese company. Remembering his Japanese language lessons, John said to him, "Hajimemashite. Doozo yoroshiku" ("How do you do? I'm glad to meet you."), as he bowed at about a 45-degree angle with his hands in his pockets. Mr. Tanaka said the same thing. John talked with them just for a short while and left. When leaving, he overheard Mr. Tanaka say to Professor Saito, "John-san wa nihongo wa joozu desu kedo, yappari amerika-jin desu ne" ("John speaks Japanese very well, but he is still after all American.").

What do you think was obviously "American" about John?

A.   John couldn't convey his polite but friendly greeting because of his halting Japanese. (See page 80.)

B.   John smiled when greeting Professor Saito. In Japan, one should not smile to a person who is socially superior. (See page 87.)

C.   John should have performed a deep (about 90 degree) bow. (See page 101.)

D.   John bowed with his hands in his pockets. (See page 71.)

32.   Invitation

For a couple of months, Brian has been working as an intern at a Japanese company. His supervisor, Mr. Kawakami, seems to have taken a personal interest in Brian. He has invited Brian out for drinks and for dinner several times but, to Brian's disappointment, has not yet asked him to his home. When Brian discussed this with friends interning under American supervisors at American companies in Japan, it seemed that Brian was the only one who had never been invited to his supervisor's home.

Why hasn't Brian yet been invited to Mr. Kawakami's home?

A. Mr. Kawakami actually does not care about Brian. (See page 100.)

B. Mr. Kawakami and his wife have been separated or divorced. Mr. Kawakami cannot clean the house or cook, so he does not want to invite Brian to his home. (See page 77.)

C. Although it is becoming more and more common for Japanese to invite people to their houses for dinner, most entertaining still takes place in public places. (See page 85.)

D. Japanese people normally wait at least a year before they invite friends home. It is presumptuous to invite those whom one doesn't know well. (See page 112.)

33.   Japanese Bath

Al was in Japan on his third business trip. One of his Japanese clients, Mr. Tamura, invited him for a weekend outing at a Japanese inn along with a few other fellow businessmen. Although Al had heard that inns serve traditional foods in the guests' rooms and that the baths, or *ofuro,* are almost a form of recreation, he had yet to stay in one.

After arriving at the inn, Al and his Japanese acquaintances were invited to use the bath. They trooped down to a changing room where they removed their Japanese-style lounging robes (*yukata*) and then walked into a steamy tiled room that contained something resembling a shallow swimming pool. It looked appealing to Al, who liked hot baths and showers. Just as he was about to ease into the bath, though, Mr. Tamura grabbed his arm.

Why did Mr. Tamura stop Al from entering the bath?

A. The water was far too hot for a foreigner. Mr. Tamura felt obligated to test it first. This Japanese custom resembles the Western practice of a host tasting the wines before serving them. (See page 88.)

B. Before entering a Japanese bath, everyone washes with soap and rinses thoroughly. Al needs to scrub down before he goes in. (See page 103.)

C. A group of Japanese women was already in the bath. Mixed bathing is fairly common in Japan, but etiquette requires that the women nod their approval before the men enter the bath. (See page 78.)

D. A *mizumushi* (literally, "water bug") was swimming around in the bath. These are large, pesky insects that bother bathers, and Mr. Tamura needed to call the management to get it out before Al could have his bath. (See page 114.)

34. Table Manners

Liz enjoys living in Japan, and she loves Japanese food. Japanese noodles are her favorite. She often has lunch at a small noodle restaurant near her downtown Tokyo apartment that's owned by a well-known *soba* (buckwheat noodle) chain. She likes the place because the food is good, the price is reasonable, and the atmosphere is pleasant. But one thing bothers Liz: the customers slurp their noodles. Liz thinks of Japanese people as polite and refined, so it's difficult for her to reconcile this image with the terrible manners of the noodle restaurant's customers.

What's going on here?

A. Japanese noodle-eating etiquette is, to Americans, unusual to say the least. In fact, Liz herself should learn to make the same noise and pick up her bowl to drink the soup that remains after the noodles have been slurped. (See page 72.)

B. Liz actually stumbled into a Taiwanese restaurant. (See page 105.)

C. This occurrence demonstrates a Japanese double standard: Japanese usually have beautiful manners only when foreigners are watching. (See page 81.)

D. Liz is neurotic. In the United States, the sound of crackers crumbling has the same effect on her. (See page 116.)

35.   Touching

Sam has been living in Japan for three months. During his daily commutes to work he would notice how Japanese people tolerate physical contact with others. Morning trains were packed, but no one seemed to mind; when walking on crowded streets, people would nearly bump into others all the time, but no one would apologize; and pushing others while trying to board the train was a daily routine for most commuters. Sam felt extremely uncomfortable, but he just assumed that Japanese people had closer body contact with one another than Americans did.

One day, Sam attended the wedding reception of his close friend, Makoto. Sam was so happy for Makoto that he hugged him in the reception line as he congratulated him. Sam realized that no one else was hugging Makoto (but then, why not, since Japanese are often in close physical contact on crowded public places?). However, Makoto's reaction was not at all what Sam had expected. Makoto nearly jumped, and Sam had never seen him look so uncomfortable and embarrassed.

Why was Makoto so embarrassed?

A. Japanese people do have close physical contact, but it's always limited to people of the opposite sex. (See page 67.)

B. As in the United States, men in Japan only hug one another when they are close friends. Makoto thought Sam was presumptuous. (See page 73.)

C. Sam had incredibly bad breath. Due to their diet, Japanese rarely have the intensely bad breath that some Americans do. Being hugged made it particularly difficult for Makoto to ignore Sam's halitosis. (See page 84.)

D. There is a difference between intentional body contact and unintentional body contact; hugging is an example of the former, and the crowded train situation of the latter. In Japan the latter occurs quite frequently but not the former. Sam wasn't aware of the difference. Makoto was surprised because he wasn't used to being hugged. (See page 106.)

36.   Waving Good-bye

Jane and her new Japanese classmate Yasuko decided to do their homework together one day in the cafeteria after their Japanese literature class. Later, they walked to the train station together, since they both commuted to school by train, but from different directions. Jane said good-bye; as Yasuko started walking toward the train that had just arrived, Jane waved her right hand in a gesture of farewell. Yasuko saw Jane waving, and she walked back to Jane and asked her what she wanted.

Why did Yasuko walk back to Jane?

A. Yasuko probably realized that she made a mistake in the homework they did together, and she wanted to tell Jane about it. (See page 68.)

B. Jane's gesture of waving good-bye means "come here" to a Japanese person. (See page 79.)

C. Jane should have used her left hand to wave good-bye; using the right hand is reserved for permanent good-byes in Japan. Yasuko wanted to explain this difference to Jane. (See page 103.)

D. Yasuko was on the wrong train platform, so she decided to come back and talk with Jane until a train came to the right platform. (See page 96.)

37.   Wedding

Alice and Jim, a couple who had recently arrived in Japan, were invited to the wedding of one of their new Japanese friends. The reception was going to be held at a well-known hotel, and about 60 people were invited. As a wedding gift, Alice and Jim bought a nice set of towels. It was rather expensive by their standards, but they thought it would be appropriate since the reception was at a fancy place.

When Alice and Jim went to the reception they were totally amazed. Although the reception started at 3:30 P.M., it was a full-course dinner! Not only that—the wedding cake was five-tiered, and large enough to feed an army. During the reception, some people gave speeches (many of them boring) and others sang songs. In addition, the bride changed her clothes three times—from her white wedding kimono to another gorgeous kimono, then to a wedding gown, and then to an evening gown. As they left the reception, all guests were given gifts. Alice and Jim were also surprised that no one else had brought any presents with them; at the entrance to the reception room, there was a desk at which the guests were leaving small, nicely decorated envelopes, but that was it.

The whole experience left Alice and Jim feeling that they should have asked for advice. When they finally discussed the wedding with a friend of the newly married couple, they found that their gift had been inadequate.

Why was their gift inadequate?

A. They were among very rich people—the huge wedding cake, the bride's changing her clothes, and the reception at a well-known hotel indicate great affluence. In Japan as in any country, rich people buy lavish wedding gifts, and Alice and Jim should have done the same. (See page 98.)

B. Alice and Jim have unpredictable, unconventional friends. The fact that they served a full-course dinner at 3:30 P.M. indicates that they lack common sense. Alice and Jim shouldn't worry if such people consider them to be stingy. (See page 74.)

C. In Japan, wedding gifts are normally expected in cash, and the amount is extremely large by American standards. A couple invited to a reception held at a famous hotel should be prepared to give 30,000 to 50,000 yen ($200 to $350). (See page 102.)

D. Towels, no matter how good the quality may be, are regarded as "cheap" gifts in Japan. Alice and Jim should have chosen a small but valuable gift that fits into a small envelope—such as silver spoons or gold chains. (See page 119.)

PART III

Commonly Misused or Misunderstood Japanese Expressions

38.   Appointment

Susan had to meet Mr. Takahashi, who had just arrived in New York to discuss some business matters. She called him at his hotel and asked for an appointment with him for the following day. Mr. Takahashi agreed and told Susan in English where they could meet. It was hard for Susan to understand what he said because his English was poor. Susan, however, caught the words "front of the hotel" and she assumed that outside of the hotel was the designated meeting place.

The next day Susan waited for Mr. Takahashi in front of the hotel, but Mr. Takahashi didn't show up. After waiting for twenty minutes, Susan decided to call his room from the front desk. There was Mr. Takahashi. When Mr. Takahashi figured out what had happened he was both amused and embarrassed.

What actually happened to Mr. Takahashi?

A. Mr. Takahashi was late; it is customary in Japan to be late for appointments. (See page 75.)

B. Mr. Takahashi forgot where he told Susan he would meet her. (See page 82.)

C. Susan went to the hotel on a wrong day and ran into Mr. Takahashi by accident. (See page 95.)

D. Mr. Takahashi's "Japanese English" caused a misunderstanding about the meeting place. (See page 117.)

39.   Carrying a Suitcase

Jane was taking a trip to Kyoto for a couple of weeks, and Mr. Yokoyama, the father of Jane's friend, Setsuko, helped her with her luggage. Mr. Yokoyama gave Jane a ride to Tokyo Station and carried her heavy luggage to the platform. When the train arrived at the platform, Jane thanked him sincerely since she couldn't have made it to the station without his help. She said with a big smile, "Hontoo ni doomo gokuroosama" ("Really, thank you so much for your trouble."). Mr. Yokoyama looked somewhat displeased. Jane saw that she must have said something wrong; immediately, she realized that she could have used a more polite ending, so she added, "Gokuroosama deshita!" That didn't seem to be any more pleasing to Mr. Yokoyama because he only nodded.

Why did Mr. Yokoyama act the way he did?

A. He had to leave quickly in order to be on time for an important appointment. (See page 104.)

B. He was exhausted by carrying Jane's heavy luggage for a long distance. (See page 91.)

C. He was offended because Jane did not bow as she thanked him. (See page 111.)

D. Jane's choice of words was incorrect. (See page 97.)

40.   Condolences

One morning Jane's host family received the news that a close relative had died. The family was shocked and grieved. Jane felt that she should express her condolences; she said, "Doomo sumimasen" ("I'm very sorry."). The family looked puzzled, as if they didn't understand what Jane meant. Later, neighbors and friends visited the family, and muttered to the family a phrase which Jane couldn't catch well but which was certainly not "Doomo sumimasen." Jane didn't understand why visitors didn't express sympathy with the family on such a sad occasion.

Why do you think Jane's host family looked puzzled when Jane expressed her condolences?

A. In a rigid society like Japan's, one should never express one's personal feelings to others. (See page 94.)

B. The relative's death is an in-group matter and so the host family didn't want an out-group member like Jane to be concerned with it. (See page 76.)

C. Jane's response was premature; she should have waited until the neighbors and friends visited with their condolences. (See page 99.)

D. Jane said "sumimasen" ("I'm sorry.") in the wrong context. The Japanese never say that in the situation in question. (See page 83.)

41. Compliment (2)

As soon as Mike arrived in Japan, he discovered the Japanese to be very nice people—they praised him wherever he went! He couldn't remember how many people had commented on how well he spoke Japanese. He was delighted each time his Japanese was complimented, and he responded with "Arigatoo gozaimasu" ("Thank you very much."). After all, he deserved it; he had never studied so hard as when he started studying the Japanese language. Mike could practice his "arigatoo gozaimasu" a great deal because the Japanese around him made many other favorable comments, such as when they saw pictures of his family. "How pretty your sister is!" "You have very nice-looking parents!" One day, however, Mike was warned by one of his friends that he shouldn't say "arigatoo gozaimasu" so often. Mike was totally puzzled.

Why should Mike not say "arigatoo gozaimasu" so often?

A. Mike's friend was tired of hearing Mike say "arigatoo gozaimasu" all the time. (See page 97.)

B. Mike's Japanese is not that good, nor are his family members that nice-looking. Japanese people are just trying to be pleasant by praising them, so he should acknowledge their kindness first, then thank them. (See page 88.)

C. It is not polite to accept praise in Japan. One is supposed to deny praise and humble oneself. (See page 113.)

D. Mike is supposed to say "doomo arigatoo gozaimasu," rather than "arigatoo gozaimasu." He wasn't polite enough. (See page 95.)

42. Congratulations

January 2 was Brian's twentieth birthday. As he was walking toward the train station to meet Lisa, who had invited him out for a birthday dinner, he saw his classmate Masao, whom he hadn't seen for a couple of weeks. Masao came up to Brian and said "Omedetoo." Brian wondered how Masao could have found out that it was his birthday; he thanked Masao and then asked him how he knew. Masao gave him a puzzled smile, and asked if Brian were going out. Brian answered that his girlfriend, Lisa, was taking him out for a birthday dinner. "Oh, I see," said Masao and added, "Sore wa omedetoo!" This time Brian was confused—why should Masao have said "omedetoo" twice since he had already thanked him?

Why did Masao say "omedetoo" twice?

A. Brian did not know that Masao used two different kinds of *omedetoo*. The first was actually a greeting used in the first few days of the new year. (See page 96.)

B. Masao forgot that he had already said "omedetoo"—perhaps he was drunk with *otoso,* the herbal sake that Japanese people drink on New Year's Day. (See page 70.)

C. Masao did not hear Brian thank him, so he thought Brian did not hear his congratulations. (See page 89.)

D. It is customary in Japan to say "omedetoo" twice. It's supposed to bring good luck. (See page 118.)

43.   Do You Want To . . . ?

Mr. Kato dropped in at Linda's apartment to say hello to her. She led him into the living room and asked, "Nani ka nomitai desu ka?" ("Do you want something to drink?") Mr. Kato seemed to be at a loss how to reply. Linda continued, "Ocha to koohii ga arimasu kedo, dochira ga nomitai desu ka?" ("I have tea and coffee. Which do you want to drink?") Mr. Kato at last opened his mouth, "Dochira demo ii desu" ("Either will be fine."). Linda decided to make two cups of coffee. She asked him if he wanted sugar and milk. He paused for a moment and said yes, hesitantly. Becoming irritated at his indecisive manner, Linda served the coffee. While Linda and Mr. Kato were talking, Linda wondered if he wanted to go to a party that night. She asked, "Konban paatii ga aru n desu kedo, issho ni ikitai desu ka?" ("There is a party tonight. Do you want to go with me?") Mr. Kato said no, with an unpleasant look. Linda was getting upset at his attitude. He didn't seem to have a pleasant time with Linda despite her kindness in offering him a beverage and inviting him to a party.

Why do you think Mr. Kato behaved in such a way?

A. Mr. Kato didn't like Linda. (See page 79.)

B. Mr. Kato was upset with Linda because she was rude. (See page 66.)

C. Mr. Kato expected food, which is always served in Japan. (See page 77.)

D. Mr. Kato is allergic to coffee. (See page 110.)

44.   Gift (4)

David was visited by Mariko, a Japanese acquaintance. She brought a nicely wrapped box with her. As she gave it to David, she said, "Tsumaranai mono desu ga, hitotsu doozo" ("It is a trivial thing, but please accept one"). David opened the box later and found two cakes in it. David was puzzled. First, Mariko said it was a trivial thing; David wondered why did Mariko say "please accept one" if there were two cakes?

Why did Mariko say, "Tsumaranai mono desu ga, hitotsu doozo"?

A. Mariko made a mistake and brought the wrong box. The box she intended to bring actually contained a trivial item. (See page 90.)

B. This is a way of being humble. The Japanese use the word *tsumaranai* to let the recipient know that the giver is not conceited about the gift; *hitotsu* does not indicate the number of items in the box but simply means "just a little bit." (See page 98.)

C. David misunderstood Mariko's Japanese. Mariko had actually said, "Tsukawanai mono desu ga, hutatsu doozo" ("These are some things I don't use, so please have two"). American students of Japanese often mix up these words. (See page 107.)

D. David simply didn't know Japanese custom. Western-style cakes are regarded as trivial in Japan; "cake" in Japanese is a collective noun so it's counted as *hitotsu* no matter how many there are. (See page 72.)

45.   Good-bye

After studying Japanese for several months, John came to Japan for the first time as a participant in the home-stay program. When John arrived in the town to which he was assigned, his host family welcomed him.

Next morning, when John was about to leave for his language class, he said, "Sayonara" to the family; they looked puzzled and asked him if he would come home that day. John said yes, but he didn't understand why they asked such a question.

When the class was over and John was on his way home, he came across his host mother on the street near their house. He greeted her, saying, "Konnichiwa"; again she looked puzzled and gave him no reply. John felt disappointed because he couldn't get across simple messages such as "good-bye" and "hello" in Japanese.

Why did John's host family look puzzled when John said "sayonara" and "konnichiwa"?

A. Japanese people never say "sayonara" and "konnichiwa" in those situations. (See page 115.)

B. They didn't understand what John said because his pronunciation was wrong. (See page 86.)

C. John didn't have to say anything in those situations because he was a member of his host family. (See page 65.)

D. They thought John was too familiar, considering it was the first day with them. (See page 81.)

46. Have a Nice . . . !

"Thank God, it's Friday!" Steve finished his work and was about to leave the office. Since during his time in Japan he had been studying the language, he thought he would try using a little Japanese. As he walked to the door, he said to his colleagues, "Yoi shuumatsu o!" ("Have a nice weekend!") Steve was curious to know how they would respond in Japanese, but they just smiled and gave no reply.

At the subway station, Steve came across another colleague, Mr. Nakamura. He had heard that Mr. Nakamura was going on a sightseeing trip to Kyoto this weekend, so he said to him, "Yoi tabi o" ("Have a nice trip."). Mr. Nakamura had the same reaction or nonreaction as the other people at the office.

Why do you think Steve's colleagues didn't respond to him?

A. Having a nice weekend/trip is a personal matter, so one should never ask or state such wishes. (See page 85.)

B. Steve did not get his message across because its sentence structure was incomplete. (See page 80.)

C. Japanese people never say, "Have a nice weekend or trip" as Steve did. (See page 108.)

D. Steve left the office when other people were still working, which is not allowed in Japanese society. (See page 99.)

47. Once More, Please

Ed and Naoko went to Professor Toda, the advisor for their university's Travel Club, to talk about the outing they had planned for the following month. After they decided on the destination and dates, Professor Toda asked them to order tickets, including *zasekishitei*. Since Ed did not catch that particular word, he said to Professor Toda, "Moo ichido itte kudasai" ("Say it again please."). Professor Toda looked at Ed quizzically for a moment but repeated the word. Ed still didn't know the word; Naoko rescued him by whispering, "That's 'reserved seat'!" Ed and Naoko left the professor's office after getting everything straight for the trip, but Ed still felt funny about the way Professor Toda responded to his question about the word he didn't understand.

What did Ed do to cause Professor Toda's response?

A. *Moo ichido itte kudasai* was the wrong phrase to use in this situation. The sentence only belongs in the classroom. (See page 105.)

B. Ed should have used the politer version, "Moo ichido itte kudasaimasen ka?" or "Moo ichido ossyatte kudasai," since he was talking to a professor. (See page 94.)

C. Ed should have heard and immediately understood the word *zasekishitei*, which is a basic word in Japanese—Professor Toda found it hard to believe that Ed's Japanese was so poor. (See page 112.)

D. In Japanese society one shouldn't ask the other person to repeat anything. (See page 87.)

48.　Please Ask

Sandy, a student at a small college in the United States, was working as an editor for the school newspaper. One day the editorial staff decided that they would like to have a special feature on U.S.–Japan relations, since the college was considering a special exchange program with a college in Japan. Sandy suggested that it might be a good idea to have Professor Ito, a visiting professor in political science from Japan, write a short article for the paper, and everyone agreed. Since Sandy had never met Professor Ito in person, she decided to request an introduction from her Japanese professor, Professor Nakahara, who knew Professor Ito. She had learned that introductions are very important in the Japanese culture. Sandy went to Professor Nakahara, explained the situation to him, and said, "Sumimasen ga, Itoosensei ni kiite kudasai" ("Excuse me, but please ask Professor Ito."). Professor Nakahara smiled and said that he'd be happy to help her out, but he also pointed out to her that she had just made a basic mistake.

What was the mistake that Sandy made?

A.　She used an incorrect verb. *Kiite kudasai* means "please listen." (See page 106.)

B.　Sandy's means of making a request was wrong. (See page 84.)

C.　Sandy left out Professor Nakahara, which was extremely rude. She should have asked Professor Nakahara to write an article, too. (See page 96.)

D.　Sandy asked for a verbal introduction. Introductions in Japan never take the form of asking someone verbally. They should be done in writing. (See page 76.)

49.   That's Right

The International Club of a Japanese university decided to have a party for foreign students studying Japanese and for Japanese students next Sunday. Tom, as a representative of American students, proposed a change of date to Ms. Sato, explaining that next Sunday would not be convenient for some American students. Ms. Sato listened to his explanation attentively and said, "Soo desu nee. Jaa, moo ichido soodan shite mimasu" ("That's right. OK, I'll consult everyone again.").

The following day, Ms. Sato called Tom and said that they had decided to have the party next Sunday anyway. Tom was annoyed because he thought Miss Sato went back on her word though she said "Soo desu nee" to his request.

What was the cause of the problem?

A. Ms. Sato is not a very straightforward person. (See page 71.)

B. Tom misunderstood a common Japanese expression. *Soo desu nee* (that's right) doesn't exactly mean that the person agrees with the other. (See page 119.)

C. Ms. Sato was definitely going to change the date, but found herself embarassingly outvoted by other students. (See page 93.)

D. Tom couldn't make his request understood clearly. (See page 78.)

50.   Where Are You Going?

On his way to visit a female Japanese student he had met the week before, Tom saw his next door neighbor, Mrs. Yamada. He greeted her by saying, "Konnichiwa. Ii otenki desu ne!" ("Hello, it's a nice day, isn't it!") Mrs. Yamada greeted him too, then asked, "Dochira e?" (Where are you going?) Although Tom thought that it really wasn't her business, he answered that he was going to Ueno Park. Mrs. Yamada became really interested, and started asking him if he were going to the zoo to see the panda, who he was going out with, and so on. Tom started getting irritated, thinking his neighbor expected him to tell her all about his private life.

Why did Tom get into the situation in which he was telling his next door neighbor about his private life?

A. Mrs. Yamada, just like other middle-aged Japanese women, is nosy. (See page 114.)

B. Most Japanese people do not consider such topics too intimate or private. Tom should expect such questions all the time. (See page 100.)

C. The question "Dochira e?" should not have been taken literally. It is simply a substitute for "How are you today?" If Tom had known this, he would not have found himself having a lengthy conversation with Mrs. Yamada. (See page 69.)

D. Tom misunderstood Mrs. Yamada's questions. She was asking for directions to Ueno Park. (See page 65.)

51. Yes, But . . .

Linda was talking with her colleague, Mr. Kato, about the company's proposal to change the circulation system. Linda told Mr. Kato in Japanese that she would like to oppose that proposal at the next meeting and explained to him her reasons. Mr. Kato listened to Linda attentively, nodding frequently and uttering "hai" or "ee." Linda saw in her dictionary that Japanese *hai* or *ee* meant yes, so she thought Mr. Kato agreed with her. Then Mr. Kato started to give his opinion, opening with the word *demo* (but). His idea turned out to be the opposite of Linda's. Linda was confused since he had said yes frequently when she was talking but didn't actually agree with her.

Which of the following best accounts for Mr. Kato's frequent utterances of "hai" and "ee"?

A. Mr. Kato was just chiming in with Linda (See page 74.)
B. Mr. Kato tried to make himself agreeable to Linda. (See page 111.)
C. Mr. Kato was teasing Linda. (See page 117.)
D. Mr. Kato wasn't paying attention to Linda while she was talking. (See page 88.)

PART IV

Handy Trivia

52.   Doggie Bag

Karen went to a steak restaurant in Japan with a good American friend, Ted. Although their host mothers were both excellent cooks, the students were extremely hungry for steak. Since beef is so expensive in Japan, steaks are seldom served. They each ordered the largest steak available at the restaurant, so quite a bit was left on Karen's plate. (Ted ate all of his serving, risking indigestion.) Since she was paying a great deal for the dinner, and the meat tasted so good, Karen decided to take the leftovers home. She called the waiter and asked for a container (a doggie bag). The waiter looked puzzled.

Why did the waiter look puzzled?

A. Japanese don't believe in eating leftovers. (See page 109.)
B. The waiter could not believe that Karen couldn't finish the steak. (See page 97.)
C. It is not customary in Japan to take leftover food home from a restaurant. (See page 90.)
D. The waiter thought that Karen didn't like the steak and felt bad; in Japan, you are supposed to eat everything if you like it. (See page 86.)

53.   Flowers (2)

Jennifer decided to visit Miyuki at the hospital. Miyuki was a fellow member of the archery club at the Japanese university Jennifer was attending. Miyuki had been in the hospital for a few days with appendicitis. Since Jennifer was told that a typical gift of nice fruits and cakes was not appropriate because Miyuki couldn't eat them, she decided to give Miyuki some flowers. Although Jennifer liked white flowers herself, she remembered that white or yellow flowers were used at funerals, so she decided instead to get a bouquet of mixed flowers. At the florist's shop, she saw some small bouquets of mixed flowers. They had green leaves and other small flowers all in one, and each one even included a small nice lotus bud. They were tied at the bottom so they seemed easy to take to the hospital, too. Jennifer bought one and headed to the hospital. When she walked into Miyuki's room and gave her the bouquet, however, Miyuki burst into laughter and Miyuki's mother simply looked startled.

Why did Miyuki and her mother have such surprising reactions?

A. The type of bouquet Jennifer bought was not appropriate for hospitalized people. (See page 99.)

B. The bouquet contained an unlucky number of flowers. (See page 118.)

C. The bouquet contained white and yellow flowers. White and yellow flowers are never to be given to a living person. (See page 64.)

D. Jennifer was not supposed to take cut flowers to a hospitalized person. Cut flowers eventually die, which symbolizes the patient's death. She should have taken a live potted plant instead. (See page 91.)

54.   Restaurant

Mary went to a department store one Sunday morning, a few weeks after she arrived in Japan. After a couple of hours of browsing, trying on clothes, and spending money, she felt tired and hungry. Since she had heard that most department stores in Japan have a floor where several inexpensive restaurants are located, she decided to try one. She walked around and finally decided on a Chinese restaurant. It was crowded, but Mary patiently waited in line. The first surprise came when she found out that no one was seating the customers; a waitress just pointed out free tables to the people in line. Finally it was her turn. She found a clear table and sat down. As soon as she sat down, a young man who looked like a college student came to her table and asked her if the other seats were free. Mary didn't feel very comfortable about saying yes, but she felt that it would be unreasonable to turn him away. He sat down at her table, called the waitress, and placed his order.

Why did the man come and sit at her table?

A. The man wanted to practice English with an American. (See page 92.)

B. At inexpensive restaurants, especially when it is crowded, it is customary in Japan to put as many guests as possible at one table—just like at university cafeterias in the United States. Mary may get more people coming to sit at her table. (See page 78.)

C. Restaurants are places where young men and women meet in Japan—just like singles' bars in the United States. The young man was attracted to Mary and wanted to start a conversation with her. (See page 70.)

D. In Japan young women are not supposed to go to restaurants by themselves, so the waitress made a mistake and seated the young man there, thinking he was with Mary. (See page 101.)

55.   Slippers

Karen came to Japan during the summer to study Japanese and to stay with a Japanese family. She was puzzled by all the slippers placed at the entrance. There was even one pair in the bathroom. They were all so pretty, but she especially liked the ones in the bathroom. That pair had some interesting Japanese letters.

She came out of the bathroom and into the kitchen where Mrs. Yamada was making dinner. Karen said, "Hi! Mrs. Yamada, look at me! I'm doing all right with these slippers. I tried to see whether I could walk with them." Mrs. Yamada's gentle smile broadened very quickly into a laugh that she tried to suppress.

Why do you think Karen's host mother's expression changed suddenly?

A. Karen had the slippers on the wrong feet. (See page 89.)

B. Karen actually *couldn't* walk around in them, and nearly broke her neck getting to the kitchen. (See page 102.)

C. Mrs. Yamada always thought Westerners had enormous feet. She thought that it was funny that Karen could fit into the slippers. (See page 116.)

D. The slippers are placed for everyone to put on after taking off shoes. However, that particular pair should be used only in the bathroom and then be left there for the next person to use. The Japanese letters mean "toilet." (See page 68.)

56.   Thermometers

When John became sick shortly after he arrived in Japan, he decided to go to a Japanese doctor. After he had given the receptionist his name and insurance information, she handed him a thermometer. John thought that he was supposed to go ahead and take his own temperature then, so he put the thermometer into his mouth. Some of the other patients in the waiting room, all Japanese, who had noticed him when he first came in, began to whisper and giggle among themselves. John felt embarrassed.

Why were the others talking about him?

A. John was wrong in thinking that he should take his own temperature. When he went into the examining room, he should have given the thermometer to the doctor. (See page 82.)

B. In Japan, taking one's temperature is considered a very personal matter. John should have stepped into the bathroom to take his temperature. (See page 68.)

C. John didn't know how the Japanese take their temperatures. When taking their temperature with conventional thermometers, they do not put them into their mouths but under their armpits. (See page 104.)

D. The sight of a foreigner taking his temperature struck the Japanese patients as interesting. (See page 73.)

Answers & Explanations

A. No. This alternative is inconsistent with the fact that there had been a lot of controversy about the issue.

B. Right. In Japan, one is expected to apologize and visit the victim of an accident, even if one is not at fault, to show his or her sincerity. In fact, one is expected to apologize whenever the other party involved suffers in any way, materially or emotionally. In many court cases, perpetrators get a lighter sentence when it is clear that they regret their actions, as reflected in their apology.

C. Wrong. A bouquet of only white or yellow flowers is not suitable for hospital visits, but it is OK to have them mixed in with other colors.

D. Wrong. He did drink apple juice and water during dinner.

A. **Correct.** In Japan, white-collar workers normally do not come home immediately after five o'clock. They either stay and work overtime, or they go out with their colleagues; on such occasions, most men do not call their wives to tell them they'll be late. Wives normally assume that their husbands are working or socializing if they do not return home by a certain time. Husbands who do call home every time they will be late may be looked upon as dominated by their wives or overly embroiled in family problems by older and more conservative Japanese colleagues.

B. There was no misunderstanding, so there is no need to apologize. Note that Keiko said the restaurant was closer to Cathy's house.

C. On the contrary. John was welcomed as a member of his host family. Therefore, he had to say something to keep up communication with them.

D. No, Tom did not misunderstand anything. Read the episode again.

A. No, not at all. The senior member who has made the invitation also pays the bills.

B. This is right. It was Linda, not Mr. Kato, who was rude because of her Japanese. The -*tai* (want to do) form should never be used when one offers something and/or invites someone to do something. In Japan, individual preferences and desires are usually not asked or stated directly; hosts typically serve drinks without requiring their guests to make a choice. When suggesting a joint activity like attending a party together, the negative question form becomes a polite invitation, as in *issho ni ikimasen ka,* much like the polite English, "Won't you go with me?"

C. On the contrary. In many organizations, getting a consensus agreement is an important part of decision making. In some Japanese companies, meetings are held frequently to achieve this result.

D. Wrong. Tadashi could be cross-eyed, but it certainly isn't a common trait of Japanese males. If John were at all observant, he would note such a physical problem and not think that Tadashi was avoiding his gaze on purpose.

A. Wrong. Although Japanese children have a lot of physical contact with one another, by the time they enter their teens touching is mostly among members of the same sex. By the time they become young adults, they have less physical contact with one another than do Americans.

B. Although there may be countries that have this custom, Japan does not. Choose again.

C. He shouldn't give up making compliments. Note that the reactions of the Japanese did in fact indicate pleasure.

D. This is right. Most Japanese people tend to avoid a direct no to a request, proposal, or invitation. A direct no indicates a strong refusal in Japanese culture, which is rude and is apt to hurt the other's feelings. In Japan, people prefer to make refusals indirectly (as seen in the section chief's noncommittal attitude), and they are also expected to understand what this sort of behavior signals.

A. Wrong. That makes no sense, because Yasuko asked Jane what she wanted.

B. You are wrong. Japanese patients would not be embarrassed to take their temperatures in front of anyone else in the waiting room.

C. Incorrect. The host mother's concern was legitimate and natural in Japan. Try again.

D. Correct. Slippers are usually placed at the entrance where you take off your shoes. You use those slippers only where the floors are made of materials other than *tatami* mattresses, usually in occidental-looking rooms and hallways. When you go to a bathroom, you must take off your house slippers and put on the slippers placed in the bathroom. When you come out, you must take off the bathroom slippers and leave them in such a position that the next person can slip them on easily. Those slippers are to be worn only in the bathroom. No matter how clean the bathroom is kept, Japanese people do not like to mix anything used in the bathroom with the things used in other areas of the house.

A. This is not true because Becky has made friends with some of the Japanese students. You should remember that whether you will be accepted or not depends largely on your approach: if *you* accept and follow Japanese cultural norms and values, you will definitely be welcomed as a friend by many Japanese.

B. Wrong. It is important to thank one's colleagues very politely, but there is no indication in this episode that Jeff didn't do so.

C. Correct. When Japanese people ask "Dochira e?" they are not expecting to hear where you are going. They are simply acknowledging your presence, and sometimes they tell you that you look very nice (therefore, you must be going somewhere) by this greeting phrase. It is similar to "How are you?" in English in that it does not expect an explanation. The most appropriate reply to "Dochira e?" is "Chotto soko made" ("Just down the way."). If Tom had answered this way, Mrs. Yamada would probably not have continued with more questions.

D. No. We see a tendency for the Japanese to form groups where we would be more individually oriented, but in actuality, dedication to the group in Japan varies a lot depending on the nature of the group and the particular context.

A. Wrong. Certain cultures assume that people who avoid the eyes of their conversation partners are dishonest, but that doesn't necessarily apply to Japanese culture.

B. Wrong. Masao may have been drinking *otoso* (although there is no indication in the text), but that is not the reason for his repeating "omedetoo." The fact that Masao said "Sore wa omedetoo" *after* Brian said that he was going out for his birthday dinner indicates that there is another reason. Try again.

C. Wrong. Inexpensive restaurants are by no means a place for meeting people of the opposite sex—not even in Japan!

D. Right. It is Japanese custom to remove one's coat before entering someone else's home, even if just for a minute. Removing one's coat does not imply that the guest intends to stay. Cathy should just grab her coat and leave with Keiko, unless she wants to talk with Keiko a little before they go out.

A. Incorrect. You cannot conclude that Ms. Sato is not truthful. She listened to Tom attentively and called him to let him know their decision the next day.

B. Wrong. Michiko may not know how badly behaved Kazuo is according to American standards, but she does know what is tolerable according to Japanese standards. It would be presumptuous for Susan to give advice.

C. You are wrong. It is not unusual for women to give flowers to each other as a friendly gesture. Men also give flowers to women; this may or may not convey a romantic message, depending upon their relationship and the situation. For example, Sarah will probably receive flowers from both male and female colleagues who see her off when she leaves Japan.

D. This is right. You should not bow with your hands stuck in your pockets! The person who does that looks lazy and impolite.

A. This is right. What is acceptable in one culture may be very rude in another. To Japanese people, slurping noodles and picking up the bowl to drink the soup are not offensive. In fact, many Japanese are dismayed when Westerners eat noodles noiselessly.

B. Wrong. It is possible but very unlikely that parents can expect their children to be absolutely perfect in any culture—even in Japan!

C. Wrong. A one-hour commute is actually considered rather convenient in Tokyo. Many men commute for two hours one way. (Most white-collar workers can afford housing only in distant suburbs of Tokyo.)

D. Wrong. Cakes of high quality are appreciated in Japan and never regarded as trivial. There are no collective nouns in Japanese. While there is no distinction between singular and plural forms in most Japanese nouns, everything can be counted using some counter/classifier.

A. Incorrect. If Yoko and her parents were not getting along well, they wouldn't have looked happy when they met her at the airport. And also Yoko probably would not have invited Meg to visit if she had serious family troubles.

B. Wrong. The text said they were close friends. Try again.

C. This is right. Responsive interjections, or chiming in (*aizuchi*), plays a crucial role in communicating with Japanese people, especially in telephone conversations. It signals that the listener is interested in the speaker and the matter being discussed. Japanese people feel uneasy if the person listening to them is silent, as Americans usually are.

D. You are wrong. Far more interesting to the patients would have been to see John doing something more "conventionally Japanese," such as eating with chopsticks.

A. This is right. Japanese *hai* or *ee* does not mean yes in this situation. It just signals that one is listening attentively, and it is used to chime in.

B. Not true. Alice and Jim's friends cannot be judged eccentric from the description of their wedding reception. For certain days considered "lucky" for weddings, hotel banquet rooms get booked quickly, so most couples must have receptions at odd hours. Since they also want to have a nice sit-down dinner reception, they settle for dinner at an unusual time.

C. Wrong. While it is important to try hard to remember people's names, and the Japanese certainly appreciate foreigners' efforts to do so, they consider it quite understandable if you can't. Japanese people themselves sometimes have difficulty remembering one another's names, and that's one reason why they carry *meishi* all the time.

D. No. Actually it would not have been terrible if Leo had made a pass, as long as he wasn't physically aggressive. Japanese men's attitudes do vary on this issue, however.

A. On the contrary, one should be punctual in Japan. Susan waited for twenty minutes; it is out of the question to keep a person waiting for such a long time.

B. Wrong. Some Japanese families *do* spoil their children just as some American families do!

C. Wrong. There is no way Mindy could have changed her clothes because Mrs. Takeda came without any advance notice.

D. Correct. Although company staff meetings in Japan can include lively discussion, group involvement in projects typically requires lots of consensus-building before formal decisions are made. One is expected to figure out that a "pointless question" or silence means reservations or disagreement. Sometimes a lone dissenter is ignored because he or she has not made the effort to get constructive criticism from workmates before formal statements are made; group approval is often secured by more informal maneuvering prior to the meeting. This process is called *nemawashi,* an important skill in Japanese society.

A. Partly true, but Mr. Brown also had a negative reaction at the business meeting. Try another alternative.

B. No. Sympathy is a feeling all humans can share; there is no in- and out-group distinction in such a situation. Note that neighbors and friends visited Jane's host family to offer condolences.

C. Right. Traditional art lessons in Japan often take the form described here. The teacher shows an example, and the students follow the example. Students are to copy the teacher until they master fundamental forms and methods. Individuality and creativity are supposed to come only after one has mastered the basics.

D. Wrong. Introductions in Japan can be either written or verbal. Try again.

A. Correct. In Japan, it is often regarded as impolite to talk about one's wishes and wants. In a situation like the one described here, the host and the hostess would not ask Kenji if he wanted to drink anything; they'd simply bring something to drink, and let the guest decide whether to drink it. (In case it is not touched, the hostess would probably bring something else later.) That's why Kenji drank some things during the dinner. Kenji probably wanted to drink something with dessert, but he didn't say what he wanted because he assumed it would be impolite to make such a request.

B. Possible but unlikely. If that's the case, Brian probably would have heard about it somewhere—either as a rumor, or from Mr. Kawakami himself over some drinks in the form of an apology for not being able to invite him to dinner at home.

C. It's hard to think that he looked unpleasant just because food was not served.

D. You're wrong. There is no indication that Mrs. Kawakami was mean; in fact, she was both apologetic and polite. Try again.

A. Wrong. It is unlikely that the Japanese police would exonerate anyone at fault, whether Japanese or American.

B. Right. Japanese restaurants, especially inexpensive ones, try to utilize all free seats. This may not be true when it is not crowded, but one should expect to eat next to other people at department store restaurants, especially on Sundays, when they are most crowded.

C. Mixed bathing is rare, except at out-of-the-way country hot springs. Inns usually have two baths, one for each sex. If there were only one *ofuro,* it would be the management's responsibility to coordinate groups so that only women or men would be in the bath at one time. If women were already there when the men entered, everyone would think that there was some kind of mistake!

D. No. She didn't misunderstand Tom. Read the passage again.

A. This is not true because Mr. Kato called on Linda to say hello. If he didn't like Linda, he wouldn't have come.

B. Right. In Japan, one waves the hand sideways with the palm facing the other person to indicate good-bye. Folding fingers and straightening them a few times with the palm facing the other person, which is the normal way of waving good-bye in the United States, indicates beckoning in Japan. Yasuko thought Jane wanted her to come back.

C. Wrong. Michiko may be having trouble dealing with Kazuo, but Susan definitely shouldn't spank him. First, Kazuo's behavior is not that uncommon in Japan; second, spanking children is not widely accepted in Japan; third, like many American parents, Japanese parents tend to be offended when others try to get involved in disciplining their children.

D. You are wrong. Rie's superiors may have been embarrassed if Sarah had given an obviously expensive gift, but flowers would not be a problem. Rie is unlikely to even mention the flowers to her boss unless he sees them on her desk.

A. No, his Japanese was correct. Professor Saito and Mr. Tanaka understood what John said and returned his greeting accordingly.

B. No. Although *yoi shuumatsu/tabi o* is not a completely finished sentence, it is very common in Japanese to use phrases without predicates.

C. Incorrect. Mrs. Uemura probably genuinely wanted to give the dolls to Kim. Offering money could be extremely insulting.

D. Right! In Japan, seeing people off is almost a ritual. You are expected to wait until the guests (or whomever you're seeing off) are out of sight; while you wait, you either wave good-bye or bow. In fact, the Youngs should have gone outside with the Yamashitas and have stayed there until the Yamashitas were out of sight. The Yamashitas, who were unfamiliar with American custom, were probably afraid that the Youngs were eagerly waiting for them to leave.

A. This is right. If Bob had been apologetic, the reactions of his boss would have been more favorable. Apologies are used very often among Japanese people to show sincerity, and to reassure others that the person recognizes responsibility and wants to cooperate. Some Japanese even believe that one should apologize for causing inconvenience to others—sometimes even when one is not really at fault!

B. Quite the contrary! Japanese men seem to enjoy seeing their friends and workmates inebriated (as long as it doesn't lead to aggressiveness or complete incoherence). Remember, Mr. Okamura was smiling, and he *did* invite Leo out again.

C. Not so—at least for noodle-eating! (Liz was certainly noticed in such a small restaurant.)

D. No. The words *konnichiwa* and *sayonara* are used as formal salutations, which hardly gives an impression of being too familiar.

A. You are wrong. John was correct in thinking he should take his own temperature before entering the examining room.

B. Perhaps, but not very likely, especially since he seemed amused.

C. Wrong. Japanese culture makes no distinction between left hand and right hand in terms of cleanliness.

D. This is correct. Making judgments about a socially superior person's proficiency is culturally inappropriate behavior in Japan. One should never sound like one is evaluating a superior. One may say, however, "Taihen benkyoo ni narimashita" ("Thanks to you, I have learned a lot") to indicate that one is impressed. Also note that the expression *kanshin shimashita* should never be used to compliment a superior.

A. Unlikely, from the fact that Jane got along well with her host family.

B. This *could* be the reason, because talking back to someone who is socially superior or criticizing someone's mistakes is considered immature in Japanese culture. But the episode tells us that Bob talked very politely to his boss, and he did not make any direct accusations. Look at the other alternatives and try again.

C. Because Becky has already made Japanese friends of her own age, this alternative is probably not true.

D. Correct. *Sumimasen* (I'm sorry) is an apology, and is never said in situations when sympathy should be expressed (someone's death, a failure, or other severe misfortune). When someone you know has lost a close relative, you say the following set phrase in a low and unclear voice: "Kono tabi wa doomo goshuushoo sama deshita" ("My condolences to you for your recent loss."). Better yet, you can let your voice trail off after saying, "Kono tabi wa doomo . . . ."

A. Wrong. Custom does not dictate that visitors should leave a host's home by nine o'clock.

B. Correct. "Please ask" sounds all right in English when someone asks for a favor. However, the -*te kudasai* form in Japanese is used as a polite *command* rather than a polite request. Sandy should have said, at least, "kiite kudasaimasen ka?" ("wouldn't you please ask"), or, better yet, "kiite itadakemasen ka" (literally, "could I please have your favor of asking for me" or "would you please ask").

C. Not true. Sam may have had bad breath, but that shouldn't cause Makoto to be markedly embarrassed. Also, despite their dietary differences from Westerners, some Japanese do have bad breath!

D. There is no indication that the host mother had written to Jane's parents first. Since the host family and Jane got along well, they would have asked her if they had suspected that her relationship with her parents had been *that* bad.

A. This is unlikely because Japanese do not have as strong a sense of privacy as do Westerners.

B. Wrong. It is true that one must try to prevent others from losing face. However, Cindy could have told her host mother how she felt about the teacher. Since Cindy's host mother had not necessarily told the teacher about Cindy, she could avoid the class without worrying about her host mother's relationship with the teacher.

C. Correct. Although some people do invite others home for dinner, home is usually reserved for resting and family life. In addition, many people feel their homes are not large enough for entertaining.

D. Doubtful. Fred and Mr. Sato had been working together, and Mr. Sato felt very self-confident concerning their project. Try again.

A. You're right. Making a complaint in Japan requires tact because a complaint could be taken as an accusation. A lie like Mrs. Kawakami's is often allowed in order to preserve the relationship between two neighbors; however, Mrs. Kawakami probably should have told her husband what she was doing.

B. No. This can't be the case. John has studied Japanese for several months so it's unlikely that he couldn't say such simple words as *konnichiwa* and *sayonara* correctly.

C. Possible, but unlikely, because Tom and his host family enjoyed their conversation so they must have understood each other. Choose again.

D. On the contrary, the traditional full-course Japanese meal is often served with the expectation that guests should eat only what they can. Since Karen is at a Western-style restaurant, the situation is slightly different; however, the waiter did not think Karen left the meat because she didn't like it. (Remember, it was the largest steak.)

A. Incorrect. The section chief was in control of the budget and did not necessarily have to seek the consensus of his subordinates because of his superior position.

B. Wrong. Smiling is encouraged because it gives a good impression. One does not have to wait until the superior smiles either.

C. Yes. Japanese college students can devote somewhat less time to studying than their American counterparts. For a few who have studied hard during high-school years for entrance examinations, club activities represent a postponed social life. Whatever the cause, these groups offer a lot of meaning and psychological gratification for their members.

D. Not true. When you don't understand what the other person says, you can feel free to ask that person to repeat it. The problem is how you ask.

A. It's possible that Mr. Tamura would be concerned about Al's reaction to the heat of the bath, but a host has no obligation to enter first. Try again.

B. Wrong. The episode does not mention Mike's ability in Japanese or the appearance of his family. Some Japanese people do try to be kind to others by praising them, but one is not expected to acknowledge their kindness.

C. Correct. Japanese of both sexes often regard personal questions as appropriate, particularly since vague answers will suffice. (Some Japanese do consider these questions too personal, however.) For instance, in response to the question about salary, one can answer, "It's so-so" or "Terrible," even if one considers oneself well-paid. One may answer the question regarding when she or he wants to get married by saying, "As soon as I find someone nice" or "I don't know yet."

D. No. If you read the episode again very carefully, you'll see that he was actually very attentive.

A. Wrong. Japanese home slippers are the same for both feet.

B. Right. Japanese do not usually give Christmas gifts to teachers or tutors. However, they *do* give gifts twice a year (once in August and once in December), called *ochuugen* and *oseibo* respectively, to those who have been helpful to them during the year such as teachers, superiors, and doctors. Gift items selected are often rather practical items, like food staples, seasoning, or soap. Those gifts are seldom opened in front of the giver, but are opened after they leave. (In fact, these days, department stores often deliver such gifts directly to the receiver's house.) It is often believed that Japanese people never open gifts in front of the giver, but that is not the case for personal gifts, such as Christmas gifts and birthday gifts, which are opened immediately.

C. Wrong. Masao did hear Brian; that's why he gave a little puzzled smile.

D. No, this is probably not the case. Yoko's parents might be "shy people," but we can't ascribe to shyness the fact that they didn't hug their daughter.

A. Very unlikely. Mariko may have made a mistake and brought the wrong box, but it couldn't have contained an item that Mariko considered "inconsequential." Japanese, as well as Americans, try to give desirable things as gifts.

B. Wrong. It is perfectly normal in Japan to drink before or after dinner as well as during it.

C. You're right. Taking leftover food from a restaurant is not a Japanese custom. Japanese people eat leftovers at home, but they do not bring them home from a restaurant.

D. Wrong. It is true that the Japanese have a lot to learn from the West and from other cultures, but others can also learn from Japan. One of the things that make a traditional art "traditional" is the way it is taught. After all, Cindy enrolled in this course presumably because she wanted to learn more about things Japanese.

A. You are right! The sound of the *kanji* character for "death" has the same sound as the character for "four." The Japanese avoid giving four of anything. Place settings and teasets always come in sets of five, and in some hospitals you will notice the absence of a fourth floor. There are many other examples of the avoidance of "four" in Japanese society.

B. Wrong. Mr. Yokoyama was probably tired, but he still would not have acted in the manner he did simply because of weariness.

C. Wrong. It is highly unlikely because social inferiors are rarely expected to critique a superior's work.

D. Wrong. It is acceptable to take cut flowers for hospital patients. It is true that some people dislike cut flowers because they eventually die, but it is also true that some other people dislike potted plants with roots because they may symbolize prolonged ("rooted") illness that will keep them in the hospital! There is another reason for Miyuki and her mother's reactions.

A. Possible, but unlikely, especially since the man went ahead and made his order without starting a conversation with her.

B. Correct. Some Japanese, especially those who are not used to foreign visitors, think hospitality includes giving away whatever they have that visitors like. They mean well, so they might be hurt if you turn them down flatly. Be aware that when you praise other people's possessions in Japan, this sort of situation can arise.

C. Wrong. The Japanese consumer economy and leisure activities are all lively and varied—a state of development hardly possible if the Japanese were indecisive! It is more likely that Kenji knew what he wanted to drink, but some other reason prevented him from saying it.

D. Wrong. It may be true that Kate is an attractive young woman and that those young men want to ask her out. However, this situation would have no relation to their asking her personal questions.

A. Wrong. It is certainly a good idea to follow one's instinct when looking for a teacher (if you are in a position to choose, that is) and Cindy could have done so. However, she might not have been able to locate a "good" teacher, since she would not know what constitutes good teaching in Japanese culture.

B. Wrong. Japanese people do discuss issues, but the Japanese style of discussion is often different from Western styles. A lively exchange of opinion is not unknown, but it rarely occurs in as "public" a forum as a staff meeting.

C. You cannot know whether Ms. Sato was definitely going to change the date. Read carefully what she said to Tom.

D. Right. One should use both hands to receive gifts in Japan. The best way of receiving something from a superior, in fact, is to extend both arms, receive the item using both hands, lift it slightly, and bow your head a little. It's a gesture of humility.

A. No, this is not true. Japanese society is not so rigid and impersonal.

B. This sounds like the right answer, but it's not. *Moo ichido itte kudasai* is a classroom phrase never used in any other situation. Even if you make it more polite by adding *-masen ka?* or by changing it to the honorific, it is still not appropriate for the situation described in the dialogue.

C. Correct. Hugging and kissing are not the way a Japanese would behave, either in public *or* in private. This doesn't mean, however, that Japanese are cold and emotionless people. They feel joy and sorrow as deeply as Westerners do, but, because the open display of emotions is not culturally approved, Japanese people tend to show their emotions in a subdued manner.

D. Wrong. In Japan people normally do not give Christmas gifts to their teachers or tutors. Besides, even if some people do give Christmas gifts, they seldom choose cooking oil.

A. Wrong. It is perfectly acceptable to wear a good pair of pants when you're receiving guests or going out. Dresses and suits are regarded as more formal and are expected on some occasions, but pants were acceptable in the situation described in this episode.

B. Correct. *Hisho,* which is translated as secretary in English, has higher status than does its American counterpart, and its job description is similar to that of an executive administrative assistant in the United States. Many large companies even have a *hisho-ka* (secretarial section), which has male as well as female employees. When Mayumi said she wanted to be a secretary, she certainly meant more than being a clerk-typist.

C. Wrong. Read the story again.

D. Wrong. The addition of *doomo* does not really make Mike's responses much more polite. Mike needs to be more polite in a different way. Try again.

A. Right. The first *omedetoo* was an abbreviation of *shinnen omedetoo* or *akemashite omedetoo,* and it meant "happy new year"; the second meant "happy birthday." The word *omedetoo* is used to express congratulations for many different occasions such as birthdays, graduations, weddings, childbirths, anniversaries, passing examinations, and certain holidays such as New Year's Day and Christmas. Brian should have responded to the first *omedetoo* with the same word (hence the puzzled smile from Masao), and to the second with *arigatoo.* The fact that Masao said "Sore wa omedetoo" after Brian said he was going out to have a birthday dinner indicates that Masao didn't know at first that it was Brian's birthday.

B. Not really. Although Americans sometimes find that their Japanese associates will do very thoughtful things for them, be assured that this kind of activity would be going on if Sally weren't around. Try again.

C. Wrong. The nature of the article was not necessarily suitable for Professor Nakahara's specialty, so there is no reason to believe that Professor Nakahara would feel left out.

D. Wrong. It is possible but is unlikely that Yasuko could make such a basic mistake when she commutes by train every day.

A. Wrong. It is doubtful that Mike's friend was tired of hearing the phrase, and even if he were, he probably would be too polite to say so.

B. Not true. Remember, Karen ordered the largest steak available at the restaurant.

C. Wrong. If Mayumi seems liberal by American standards, she probably is quite liberal by Japanese standards. A "traditional" woman would probably intend to work for a few years and then quit when she gets married; she would certainly not consider having a "career."

D. Correct. The expressions, *gokuroosama,* and the even politer version, *gokuroosama deshita,* are usually used by a superior to an inferior when the former thanks the latter (normally when the inferior has done what was expected). In this situation Jane should have said, "Doomo arigatoo gozaimashita," since her friend's father is older than she.

A. Not true. Alice and Jim's friends are probably well-to-do, but they may not be rich. A wedding is a big event in Japan, and ordinary middle-class people spend thousands of dollars for the wedding. Similarly, it is customary to have a large and elaborately decorated wedding cake. Only part of it is real cake; the rest is decorated cardboard that is used for other weddings.

B. Correct. Unlike in the United States, where the giver presents a gift with pride, saying things such as "I hope you like this," a gift is presented with deprecating words in Japan. In this context the word *hitotsu* should not be taken literally.

C. This is doubtful because the section chief had a month to consider the proposal.

D. Wrong. It is true that some men leave their families in Japan when their assignment is as short as a year, but that is usually only when they have school-age children who need to remain in Japan for their educations. Some companies do prefer to send husbands overseas alone at the beginning of their assignment, but wives are encouraged to join them later.

A. Right. The bouquet that Jennifer bought was meant to be an offering to a Buddhist altar. You can tell such bouquets apart from others because they are made to be seen only from one angle (shaped flat) and they always have green, hard leaves in the back. If you see a lotus bud or pod, you can almost always be assured that the bouquet is for a Buddhist altar.

B. Wrong. Although it is possible that the Yamashitas were jealous enough to feel resentful, the Youngs would have noticed the tension the night before.

C. No. There is no prescribed time for expressing condolences—if anything the sooner the better. Try another alternative.

D. Not true. When people leave the office is important, but departure time would not influence the response to a casual comment. Furthermore, Mr. Nakamura had also left the office or else Steve couldn't have seen him at the station.

A. Wrong. Mr. Kawakami does care about Brian, or else he wouldn't have invited Brian out for drinks and dinners.

B. Incorrect. Some Japanese people are very curious about foreigners and ask personal questions, especially when they first meet, but they *do* consider the topic of dating rather private and don't expect detailed answers.

C. Wrong. It is true that an international experience often brings about marvellous changes in young people. However, it is unlikely that anyone could change so dramatically in six months or so.

D. Correct. Modesty is highly valued in Japanese society. Denial of compliments is a good example of this cultural value. Young people today may respond in the American way to compliments like "you look nice in that dress" (though compliments like this are not as popular in Japan as they are in America). But they usually add, "but I bought this at a bargain!"

A. Wrong. A negative observation is equal to canceling the compliment in any culture.

B. This is right. Blowing one's nose in front of others is not considered good manners in Japan. Japanese people tend to blow their noses out of sight of others, or, if this isn't possible, they at least turn away before blowing their noses. They also use disposable tissues, not handkerchiefs!

C. Not really. A "medium" bow was quite appropriate. But you're on the right track. Try again.

D. Wrong. There is no such social rule. Young women may eat out by themselves if they wish to. Besides, the waitress did not seat anyone at this restaurant.

A. Wrong. It is not customary to drink tea before going out to eat in Japan.

B. Wrong. She did get to the kitchen unscathed. There's no indication in the story that she was stumbling. Try again.

C. You're right. If you're invited to a wedding reception and attend it, you should be prepared to give in cash *at least* the amount that covers your meal—20,000 yen per person may be a good amount for a fancy hotel reception. (Never give 40,000 yen per couple, however, since it is considered an unlucky number; give 30,000 or 50,000.)

D. Possible, but unlikely. Read the passage again, and you will see that Mayumi asked John if he thought she could not do the job. This indicates that she pronounced the word "secretary" clearly.

A. Wrong. It is true that Japanese youngsters are expected to behave themselves outside their homes, but that does not seem sufficient to explain the situation. It is not likely that anyone could behave *that* differently, especially in personality and performance in school.

B. Quite correct. The unwashed foreigner hopping into the communal bath is the innkeeper's nightmare. (Scrubbing down before bathing is also semi-recreational; among family members, and close friends, washing one another's back is an expression of intimate friendship.)

C. Wrong. One may use whichever hand one likes to wave good-bye in Japan. Using the right hand or left hand makes no difference.

D. Incorrect. Mrs. Uemura was not intending to sell her work at all. Asking the price of the dolls either would anger Mrs. Uemura or hurt her feelings.

A. Possible, but unlikely. There was no mention of such an appointment in the text.

B. Doubtful. Note that Fred was calling Mr. Sato, which suggests his own interest in the subject.

C. You are right! Many modern Japanese medical facilities now have electronic thermometers, which are indeed put into the patient's mouth by the nurse. The traditional way to take one's temperature in Japan, however, is to place the thermometer under one's armpit, and that is why the patients found John's way so amusing. (People get bored with nothing to do in Japanese waiting rooms, too!)

D. Susan should not interfere in this situation, but she would be overreacting if she ended her association with Michiko unless some other reasons make Susan believe Michiko is not worth having as a friend. Kazuo's behavior is not that outrageous, if not very common, in Japan.

A. You're right. This sentence, which every student of Japanese learns, is unfortunately an expression that is used only in instructional contexts, and not to one's teachers and other social superiors under any circumstances. When you want the speaker to repeat a word or phrase, use "Ha?" or "Hai?" (or, if with close friends, "E?").

B. Wrong. Read the episode again; it's a *Japanese* noodle shop.

C. Wrong. Japanese law and customs have no special rule concerning accidents involving children.

D. Wrong. Japanese names are very difficult; even Japanese people cannot always read proper names correctly. (That's another reason why they carry *meishi* all the time!) They certainly do not expect foreigners to be able to read every Japanese name in *kanji*.

A. No, Sandy used the correct verb. *Kiite kudasai* means both "please listen" and "please ask."

B. This doesn't account for the section chief's noncommittal attitude; he could flatly reject Phyllis's proposal if he didn't like Phyllis.

C. Extremely unlikely. Even the most aggressive businessman in Japan is allowed to have a headache once in a while. Mr. Kawakami's promotion would not be sidetracked because of one headache, so he would not be afraid that people would find out that he had been ill.

D. Correct. Japanese people do not have as much intentional body contact as do Americans. Physical contact on crowded trains and streets is a totally different situation because the context is impersonal, and considered unavoidable. Intentional physical contact in public, like walking arm-in-arm, is typically found only between young girls and among intoxicated businessmen. Hugging is even rarer.

A. Incorrect. Mrs. Uemura probably was being very polite, but she also was serious about giving the dolls away to Kim. (It is often said that Kyoto people insist on offering things expecting to be declined, but that is an exception, and a somewhat dubious one at that.)

B. Right. Seniority is crucial in deciding the level of formality, no matter how small the age difference may be. Especially in a highly structured group like a university club or a company, even a one-year difference is significant.

C. Wrong. It is true that *tsukawanai* and *tsumaranai* sound a little alike, and that American students often mix up *hitotsu* and *hutatsu*. However, Japanese would not give gifts to anyone because they do not use them, and Mariko did actually say *hitotsu*. Try again.

D. No. Some supervisors do not like to be talked back to by their subordinates, part-time or not, but there is nothing particularly Japanese about such preferences. Try another alternative.

A. Wrong. Women's status is still low in Japan, but today there is an increasing number of women who have professional careers.

B. You are wrong. Red is a color used to offer congratulations in Japan; red roses and carnations are often seen at a Japanese wedding, for example. In contrast, white flowers are often seen at funerals.

C. This is right. Steve's attempt to translate the English expression "Have a nice X" directly into Japanese is wrong because there is no expression like that in Japanese. (There is one exception, "Yoi otoshi o" ["Have a nice year."]. Japanese say instead, "Jaa, mata raishuu" ("See you next week.") for "Have a nice trip." In most languages, idiomatic, informal expressions are often untranslatable.

D. Incorrect. It was fine for Tom to have an extra serving after his hosts offered it, if he had been still hungry.

A. Wrong. There are some people who don't eat leftovers in every country and Japan is no exception, but the Japanese are not necessarily more wasteful than other nationalities; they do eat leftovers.

B. Wrong. She certainly should not judge all Japanese by this particular group, but there is no indication that they are a particularly atypical, impolite group of people. "Polite" groups of people do often ask questions like the ones Kate was asked.

C. Correct! If you enjoy social drinking, save this answer and refer to it until you have it memorized.

D. Not true. There *are* linguistic styles characteristic of women's speech in Japanese. These styles include formality and politeness, and women tend to talk more formally and politely than men. However, such differences are irrelevant here, because, even if Becky were a man, she would still have to use formal speech. Try again.

A. Correct! It is considered good manners for guests not to accept an offer at first. Therefore, hosts try to repeat an offer until they are sure that their guests really want to decline. Tom could have refused their offer politely by saying, "Arigatoo gozaimasu. Demo moo onaka ga ippai desu kara . . . ." ("Thank you, but I'm already full."), without hurting their feelings.

B. No. Jane's Japanese was grammatically correct and even polite, so there must have been something wrong other than structural precision. Try another alternative.

C. We don't know from the episode that Bob's boss doesn't like foreigners and bullies Bob. Therefore, it is hard to describe this single incident as "bullying," nor can we generalize it as xenophobic.

D. Very unlikely. When one is allergic to something, one would probably say so. In this episode, however, Mr. Kato said that "either will be fine" when he was asked whether he preferred tea or coffee.

A. Not so. There is nothing about martial arts clubs per se that sets them apart in their social activities, and the samurai tradition emphasizes discipline and moderation.

B. Probably not. Mr. Kato opposed Linda, after all. Try another alternative.

C. Unlikely. True, Jane should have bowed in addition to smiling, but the lack of a bow itself should not have elicited this reaction from Mr. Yokoyama.

D. Correct. It is very common for Japanese people to disparage themselves and their family members as an expression of humility. Tomio's father must be extremely proud of his son; the fact that Tomio was smiling as his father criticized him indicates that Tomio understood what was going on.

A. You're right. *Meishi* are very often regarded as one's "face." You should not write directly on someone else's *meishi,* or put them in your back pocket even in a wallet; when you sit down, you end up sitting on the *meishi.* Jeff should have put the cards in his coat pocket or in a brief case. Jeff should also buy a business card wallet for such occasions.

B. Extremely unlikely. There is no indication that Mrs. Kawakami is completely ignored by her husband. Besides, there has not been any epidemic of paranoia reported among Japanese housewives—yet.

C. *Zasekishitei* is not an everyday word, although it may be a basic vocabulary item. An average professor would not be surprised if an American student did not know the word.

D. Wrong. Japanese people who do invite friends home for entertaining do so shortly after they get to know each other. There is no need to wait for a year.

A. No. Other people also thought his book was good; notice the favorable reviews.

B. Wrong. Japanese people *do* compliment one another, and some of the compliments are in fact regularly used, familiar phrases.

C. Correct. Regardless of Mike's true ability in Japanese and the attractiveness of his family members, Mike is not supposed to accept praise with straight thank yous. The Japanese normally deny such compliments by saying, "Iie, iie" ("No, no."). This act is a way of showing one's humility. There are some Japanese today who do not believe in negating compliments if people are sincere and the person praised is happy about it. They say one should be honest about one's feelings and should express one's pleasure. On the other hand, there are those who think that such a response is conceited. Many Americans feel uncomfortable, however, following the tradition of denying compliments. It may be a good compromise to say "Arigatoo gozaimasu," but add some statements such as "but I still need to improve a great deal," or "but Japanese is so hard that I must study much harder to be really good." These responses indicate that you are also being humble.

D. This is unthinkable.

A. Mrs. Yamada may be a nosy person, but we can't tell from this dialogue alone. Try again.

B. Correct. As a rule, in Japan college students are not regarded as independent adults, and host parents expect a thank-you letter from their students' parents for providing alternative parental care. Host parents feel particularly responsible for the well-being and safety of girls, so a letter from home is expected.

C. Wrong. Cathy should not interpret Keiko's taking off her coat as a sign that Keiko intended to stay.

D. No organisms larger than microbes are known to invade Japanese baths, with the possible rare exception of wild monkeys in the countryside of northeastern Japan. (*Mizumushi*, by the way, means "athlete's foot.")

A. This is right. John should have said "Itte kimasu" or its politer form "Itte mairimasu," meaning "I'm leaving now" (literally, "I'll go and come back."), when leaving the house and "Tadaima" ("I'm home.") when coming back from school. Japanese words like *konnichiwa* and *sayonara* are popular with Americans, but the usage of these words is very different from the English "good afternoon" and "good-bye." First, *konnichiwa* is never said to one's own family members. Remember that John was welcomed as a member of his host family. The same is also true of *sayonara. Sayonara* is used with people other than family members when one will be parting with them for a long time. This is why the host family asked John if he would come back that day.

B. This is unlikely because Yoko's parents welcomed both Yoko and Meg warmly. It's hard to imagine that refraining from hugging indicates anger. Some people might want to spend such a special moment in relative privacy, but this wish has nothing to do with Japanese custom.

C. Wrong. If those awkward moments had been that taxing, the evening would not have gone so nicely and the Yamashitas would not have promised to get together again soon.

D. Wrong. There are some people in *any* society who fit that description, but they are a very small minority at most.

A. Right. Small children, especially boys, are often not well-disciplined at home in Japan. Many "bad" behavior patterns are simply regarded as typical, and both parents and visitors just try to ignore them. When the children's behavior gets too disruptive (often intolerable according to American standards), parents then take action (like sending the child to his or her room). Japanese parents believe children eventually learn how to behave—which they do when they are older.

B. Wrong. Few young people can afford apartments larger than a one-room apartment.

C. Wrong. It is true that Westerners' feet are typically longer than Japanese feet, but it's unlikely that Mrs. Yamada would laugh about it, especially since the slippers fit Karen.

D. Highly improbable. If Liz were that neurotic, she wouldn't have the sense of adventure and emotional flexibility required for Americans to enjoy Japan. Try again.

A. Wrong. If Mrs. Takeda made a mistake, she could have told Mindy so. Besides, it is rather unlikely to make a mistake when the box is an extremely heavy one.

B. Wrong. Many women may be unhappy about their husbands' outings and irregular schedules. Nevertheless they are typically resigned to their husbands' work demands.

C. No. He was very attentive to her proposal. It is not Japanese style to tease someone in that fashion.

D. This is right. Misunderstanding occurred because of Mr. Takahashi's misuse of *gairaigo* (meaning Japanese words borrowed from Western languages). Mr. Takahashi used the word "front" in the Japanese sense, *furonto,* "front desk" of the hotel. One should be careful when using or interpreting *gairaigo.* Not all borrowed foreign words used in Japanese are identical in meaning to their original usage.

A. Not so. Phone service in Japan is as good as in the United States.

B. Probably no. There are some unlucky numbers in Japan, but the story doesn't mention the number of flowers in the bouquet.

C. Correct. According to Japanese custom, a speaker should not look directly into someone's eyes, especially if the other person is an elder, a superior, or a stranger. These days some young people have started imitating American-style direct eye contact, so not every Japanese acts like Tadashi. However, not looking into one's eyes while talking is no indication of dishonesty in Japan.

D. Wrong. There is no such custom as saying "omedetoo" twice on one's birthday for good luck.

A. Wrong. It is true that many Japanese (especially older people) believe that the younger generation does not behave as politely as their elders do. However, older people would probably ask her similar questions.

B. Correct! Although Tom thought *soo desu nee* meant "That's right" in English, *soo desu nee* in this case just indicated that the hearer understood what the speaker wanted and was going to give an answer, or, depending upon the intonation, that the speaker was hesitant to give the answer. Therefore, the follow-up response will just as likely be "Yappari yamemashoo" ("No, I won't.") as "Jaa soo shimashoo" ("OK. Let's do.").

C. We don't know from the episode if he made such a noise when blowing his nose. Try another alternative.

D. Not true. There is no such custom in Japan as giving metal things as wedding gifts. Try again.

TRAVEL AND CULTURE BOOKS

"World at Its Best" Travel Series
Britain, France, Germany,
Hawaii, Holland, Italy, Spain,
Switzerland, London, New York, Paris

International Herald Tribune
Guides to Business Travel in Asia and
Europe
New York on $1,000 a Day (Before Lunch)
Mystery Reader's Walking Guides:
London, England
Everything Japanese
Japan Today!
Japan at Night
Japan Made Easy
Discovering Cultural Japan
Bon Voyage!
Business Capitals of the World
Hiking and Walking Guide to Europe
Where to Watch Birds in Britain and
Europe
Living in Latin America
Frequent Flyer's Award Book
Guide to Ethnic London
Guide to Ethnic New York
European Atlas for Travelers
Health Guide for International Travelers
Travel Guide to British/American English
Chinese Etiquette and Ethics in Business
Korean Etiquette and Ethics in Business
Japanese Etiquette and Ethics in Business
How to Do Business with the Japanese
Japanese Cultural Encounters

Passport's Regional Guides of France
Auvergne, Provence, Loire Valley,
Dordogne, Languedoc, Brittany, South
West France

Passport's Regional Guides of Indonesia
New Guinea
Bali
Spice Islands

Passport's Travel Paks
Britain, France, Italy, Germany, Spain

Passport's China and Asia Guides
All China; Beijing; Fujian; Guilin,
Canton & Guangdong; Hangzhou &
Zhejiang; Hong Kong; Nanjing &
Jiangsu; Shanghai; The Silk Road; Tibet;
Xi'an; The Yangzi River; Yunnan; Egypt;
New Zealand; Australia; Japan; Korea;
Thailand; Malaysia; Singapore

Passport's India Guides
Bombay and Goa; Dehli, Agra and
Jaipur; Burma; Pakistan; Kathmandu
Valley

Southwest China off the Beaten Track

On Your Own Series
Brazil, Israel

"Everything Under the Sun" Series
Spain, Barcelona, Toledo, Seville,
Marbella, Cordoba, Granada, Madrid,
Salamanca, Palma de Majorca

Passport's Travel Paks
Britain, France, Italy, Germany, Spain

Exploring Rural Europe Series
England & Wales, France, Greece,
Ireland, Italy, Spain, Austria, Germany,
Scotland

"Just Enough" Phrase Books
Just Enough Dutch
Just Enough French
Just Enough German
Just Enough Greek
Just Enough Italian
Just Enough Japanese
Just Enough Portuguese
Just Enough Scandinavian
Just Enough Serbo-Croat
Just Enough Spanish
Multilingual Phrasebook
Let's Drive Europe Phrasebook

Passport Maps
Europe; Britain; France; Italy; Germany;
Holland, Belgium & Luxembourg;
Scandinavia; Spain & Portugal;
Switzerland, Austria & the Alps

PASSPORT BOOKS
a division of *NTC Publishing Group*
4255 West Touhy Avenue
Lincolnwood, Illinois 60646-1975